What People Are Saying

I didn't know what was going on with me, I just knew that I wasn't getting anything done. I could spend half a day staring at the ceiling (wall, window, speck in the carpet) and my life was slipping away. I would joke about it:

"I went somewhere, don't know where. I just wish I would take myself with me. I love to travel!"

Spiritual addiction! I learned about it from Rose Rosetree.

I started doing 20 Daily Minutes of Technique Time, Tops. I've gotten more of my life back. Things are getting done. Thanks, Rose.

— Melodee Myers, Salt Lake City, Utah

When I first reached out to Rose, I was meditating 50-60 hours a week on top of other healing practices. I had $500 to my name and I was perpetually single, seriously ill, and suicidally miserable.

She had a radical suggestion that probably saved my life: living a regular human life is the most important way to grow as a person and way less dangerous than those extreme practices.

Fast forward a few years and I spend minutes a day on my spiritual growth. And the rest of the time, I do satisfying work that pays me well in in a city I love. I'm also freelance writing, learning guitar, dancing, and falling in love.

Rose's work is revolutionary in its commonsense approach to personal growth... and the fact that it actually works. Let's face it, few of the other things I tried ever worked for long.

— Eric Vaughan, Washingt̶o̶n̶ D̶.C̶.

Spiritual addiction had caused a lot of my problems, but I didn't know what "spiritual addiction" even meant until I encountered Rose. She recommended that I cut way back on my Technique Time to see if it made a difference in my life. I told Rose that my only concern was how strangely heavy my body felt whenever I stopped all that meditating.

Her response? "That's just you being in your body!"

OK, that made sense.

It took me a while to adjust to being in my body, and a few years to completely inhabit my life. Shortly after I stopped spending so much time on that inward journey, my depression disappeared completely.

— Howard West, Cambridge, Massachusetts

Because of being raised under communism, where society is valued over the individual, I can totally relate to the need for using time for personal development.

For me, the surface of life seemed like the only reality. Soon after I first started learning from Rose, I realized how frozen I felt.

Communism, especially, made it very hard for me to even *get* the idea of personal growth. Fast-forward to now, and I am loving my freedom to grow. It makes such a difference, using 20 Daily Minutes of Technique Time, Tops, in the way Rose explains it.

Now I am choosing a path of personal growth, and life has opened up for me. Words cannot express my gratitude.

— Elena Ivanova, Silicon Valley, California

Spiritual addiction nearly cost me my career. I was so busy being "spiritual" and seeking my "path" that I saw my job (a flexible, well-paying job) as an inconvenience. I hated it. My relationships at work were terrible, and I was not respected.

Since cutting my Technique Time to 20 daily minutes, I have found a big difference. Not only do I have more time for the rest of my life; also I am enjoying those things that I choose to do.

No longer do I feel the need to "Look for my path." When things don't work out, I'm done with making excuses that, "It must be because I'm not supposed to do that." This has been liberating.

Even my relationships at work have changed for the better. I suppose that, to other people, I seem more present. I am enjoying my job much more.

— Jasmine Lee, Brisbane, Australia

When Rose gently introduced me to the concept of spiritual addiction, I was spending a significant amount of time on self-improvement but didn't realize it.

Initially I had some resistance to the idea of limiting my "Technique Time." To me, I was doing this to be a better person so that I could help others.

Once I consistently began a routine of 20 minutes a day, I noticed I could prioritize at a new level. Now I focus more attention on the people I love and care about. I am quicker to take action when needed, rather than just think about why something has happened. I am also more effective when helping others. To sum it up, I appreciate and enjoy my life more.

— Pat Wright, Bowie, Maryland

Usually I start a new year by stating "I'm glad that year's over," but not this time. Last year goes down in my personal history as one of my best ever (and last year included a lot of hardships) because I got my spiritual path back on track. I know there is lot to be done yet, but it fills me with excitement and not dread.

— Katriina Karvonen, Helsinki, Finland

ENERGY HEALING SKILLS FOR THE

AGE OF AWAKENING

The
New
Strong

STOP FIXING YOURSELF--AND ACTUALLY

ACCELERATE YOUR PERSONAL GROWTH

(Rules & Tools for Thriving in the "Age of Awakening")

Rose Rosetree

Women's Intuition Worldwide
Sterling, Virginia

The New Strong

STOP FIXING YOURSELF---

AND ACTUALLY ACCELERATE YOUR PERSONAL GROWTH!

(Rules & Tools for Thriving in the "Age of Awakening")

PUBLISHER'S CATALOGING-IN-PUBLICATION

(Prepared by The Donohue Group, Inc.)

Names: Rosetree, Rose.

Title: The new strong : stop fixing yourself-- and actually accelerate your personal growth : (rules & tools for thriving in the "Age of Awakening") / Rose Rosetree.
Description: Sterling, Virginia : Women's Intuition Worldwide, LLC, [2016] | Series: Energy healing skills for the Age of Awakening ; [book 4] | Index available in online supplement.
Identifiers: ISBN 978-1-935214-41-0 | ISBN 978-1-935214-43-4 (ebook)
Subjects: LCSH: Self-actualization (Psychology) | Consciousness. | Energy medicine. | Spiritual healing. | Intuition. | Aura. | Self-help techniques.
Classification: LCC BF637.S4 R67 2016 (print) | LCC BF637.S4 (ebook) | DDC 158.1--dc23

ISBN: 978-1-935214-41-0   LCCN: 2016904637

Please direct all correspondence and inquiries to

Women's Intuition Worldwide, LLC
116 Hillsdale Drive, Sterling, VA 20164-1201
rights@rose-rosetree.com
703-450-9514

Visit our website: www.rose-rosetree.com

Dedication

WITH BEST WISHES FROM ROSE !

Living in this new Age of Awakening,
you can get strong, The New Strong.
To make your sweetest dreams come true,
start with your true empowerment,
real as the taste of salt.

Tiny changes can alter so much.
Discover when to do a bit less,
when to do a bit more,
and which is your best vibrational frequency
to do anything.

Growing stronger, humanly strong,
you can awaken as never before.

Table of Contents

Online Supplement at www.rose-rosetree.com

Glossary — Annotated Contents — Index

PART ONE

Today's New Energy Awareness

"Eat your breakfast so you'll do your best at school. You need that energy."

When you were a kid, didn't you hear things like that?

Only today's energy awareness is far more involved. Today we're bandying around energy talk like it's second nature.

- "I like her energy, don't you?"
- "But her friend has such bad vibes. Did you notice?"
- "Lately I've been feeling stuck. I think maybe I need to strengthen my Root Chakra."

Yes, that's how many of us talk these days. Somehow we've become really good at speaking the language of energy. You may even have a hunch that energy awareness could help you get more out of life. (And I think you'd be right about that.)

Today's new energy sensitivity is good. It *feels* good. Only let's keep in mind, all that energy awareness has a negative side. For example, have you heard people talking like this?

- "His energy is so bad, I'm afraid he's toxic. Maybe an energy vampire!"
- "All day long I keep working to ground myself. Except I'm not sure it is making much of a difference."

And what about problems that don't seem to have any connection to energy? Problems like:

- "It's crazy, how hard I've been working on myself lately. I tell myself that I'm making progress. But am I? Sometimes I'm not so sure."

- ～ "How come my relationships seem to be getting worse, not better?"
- ～ "Why am I having this brain fog? It scares me. And I worry, what if other people notice?"
- ～ "Negative emotions are driving me nuts. It's like I can't shake them."

Could be, pesky problems like these indicate that something different is happening to make normal life today no longer quite... normal. Could be, these problems are also related to today's new energies.

Could be, something very important has shifted energetically for all human beings — even if otherwise observant people like you didn't happen to notice, not exactly.

Do you remember what it was like before December 21, 2012? Leading up to that date, the media broadcast it like a big story, how the Mayan calendar was due to end, and something was supposed to change, but who knew what?

How big a story was this, back in the day? More than half a year in advance, Reuters took a survey and found that 1 in 10 people believed that, punctually on December 21, 2012, the world would end.

Do you remember? What did you think would happen? Were you disappointed afterwards, when you woke up as usual and nothing seemed different? After all that hype fizzled, did you give that Mayan calendar even one more thought?

How quickly most of us moved on! But something big really did happen, a new **AGE OF AWAKENING.** I'm convinced, this has been the biggest deal of our time.

You wouldn't know it from media coverage. Or non-coverage. Yet moving into this new era matters more than Jennifer Lawrence's hottest movie in 2012 ("The Hunger Games"); or following the Kardashians and Bruce Jenner (later known as Caitlyn Jenner);

or knowing which star won the Oscar for Best Actor in a movie. (That was Daniel Day-Lewis playing President Lincoln, as you may recall if you're a fan.)

THE SHIFT that happened for keeps in 2012 has impacted your life more than any performer, any award. Mattered more than who won the World Series or the World Cup. That seemingly unremarkable shift mattered far more, long term, than anything in politics, either. No kidding.

Well, if what happened was such a big deal, why don't most people know? Couldn't it have gone viral as a video?

No, because it just couldn't. A shift this big and this different and this subtle doesn't show on the surface of life. Learning about it takes curiosity, an open mind, and practicality (rather than gullibility).

Because you have all that, you can be among the first to benefit from what has changed.

Here's a summary. Underlying your life experiences and mine, the entire planet has begun to operate differently, giving people effortless access to higher vibrational frequencies. Awareness is more fluid, making personal growth faster than ever before, so long as we play by the new rules.

You know how certain rules are needed on a highway, making it safer to drive at high speeds? Similarly the age we're in now comes with important new rules about living, rules that we break at our peril. Rules that nobody told you about. Until now.

CHAPTER 1

How the New Vibrational Rules Crept up on You

It's not just you and your friends. Have you noticed how, since about 1980, nearly everybody has grown more aware of energy?

With each passing decade, so much more energy talk! Hey, have you ever wondered, *why* did this happen?

Is it just because some people have written books and taught seminars? Did millions of people all over the world take a Reiki workshop or learn EFT (tapping), and that's what caused all the big changes? Could it be just a coincidence that so many of the seven billion people on earth went on a quest around the same time that you did?

Something happened, for sure. Because suddenly just about everyone is speaking energy talk. It's way more than a fad. We have passed a tipping point.

Well, what if your personal quest was a result, not a cause? Maybe today's new energy sensitivity didn't come from self-help teachers but, instead, *caused* them to teach as they did.

Maybe we human beings became energy sensitive because of something bigger, a vibrational shift to the entire planet that began to build over the centuries, accelerated even more rapidly starting in the 1980's, then clicked into place on that fateful day in 2012. After that once-in-an-eon change, all of humanity shifted into this Age of Awakening.

And then, energetically, the rules changed for us all. Which rules? Only the rules that underlie your personal growth, how strong you feel, how you overcome problems, which friends you make, which friends you keep, what the heck is going on with your love life, how your career progresses, and whether or not you fulfill your dreams.

Think I'm exaggerating? Discover what a difference it makes when you get skills for living by today's new rules. Still being yourself, with your basic belief system. Definitely you, just like always. Except that now you're following the new rules. And consequently you're able to fulfill your desires better than ever before. That's your opportunity, anyway.

Skills Based on Energetic Literacy

Just because energy talk has gone mainstream, does that mean our conversations are smart? All too often, it's energy interest without much knowledge, like casual chit-chat or even gossip.

Seems to me, if we're to thrive in this new age, we need new energy *healing* skills. The basis for that is a second set of skills, designed for energy *reading*. And, of course, both these skill sets would need to work in a way that follows the new rules for this Age of Awakening.

You're ahead of me here, aren't you? This Rose Rosetree thinks she's got both sets of skills.

Okay, that's right. It has taken decades and, yes, I am one of the people who has managed to do this. Which brings us to the special **ENERGY HEALING SKILLS** that you will be learning as part of this book. It helps that I work in the emerging field of **ROSETREE ENERGY SPIRITUALITY (RES)**.

This form of energy healing emphasizes emotional and spiritual development. Distinctive skill sets are involved, including 12 Steps to Cut Cords of Attachment® and Vibrational Re-Positioning®. And, ta da: certain skills for energy healing that have been developed just for this book!

RES also depends upon **ENERGY READING SKILLS.** That means a kind of literacy, like reading this paragraph now, only about energy. **ENERGETIC LITERACY** means accurately reading the human energy field in detail. Just as right now you are reading this paragraph.

With word literacy, you are not kinda sorta sensing how maybe there might be meaning to the squiggly shapes on the page. Long ago, you mastered reading words.

How hard is that for you now? A snap! Once you got those word literacy skills, reading became a snap. Well, it can become just as comfortable to read energies accurately. And not just random energies but highly informative energies about what makes a person tick, reading the **HUMAN ENERGY FIELD** or **AURA.**

Which kind of aura reading will be used to help you here? I call it "energetic literacy" because it's different from aura reading as practiced either by psychics or by experts at energy medicine (like Reiki or Eden Energy Medicine).

For energetic literacy, I use a skill set called "Aura Reading Through All Your Senses®." This has been taught to thousands of people worldwide. Here you'll benefit from all the years I spent developing this skill, then applying it to energy healing for emotional and spiritual growth. In this book I won't be teaching you how to develop energetic literacy, because we have plenty else to do. But...

Along the way, I've learned some information which I will be sharing with you: practical discoveries related to the new rules of this age.

Thanks to this background, I can help you to end many kinds of suffering that may *feel* like same-old, same-old grunge. Yet really these problems result from new challenges, related to earth's new vibrational rules.

To learn about all this, I've been in the right place at the right time, facilitating 10,000+ RES sessions with clients. The combination of knowledge and skills I'll be sharing with you were developed on demand. Real people needed real results. And got them.

Like me, you've had a front row seat during earth's rapidly accelerating (yet subtle) vibrational changes that clicked into place on December 21, 2012. This Age of Awakening matters enormously for every human being's quality of life, yet few of us have stopped to think about it. Most of us have been kept so busy with coping and adjusting, we haven't paused to ask ourselves this simple question...

What Really Happened with The Shift?

Both spiritually and psychologically, deeper energies used to be hidden from view. Now they are hidden no more. In fact, these subtle energies are almost too noticeable. All that unlimited access has given rise to problems — tricky problems that this book will help you to solve.

Every day you hear so much energy talk, but does that necessarily make your life better? Today's new rules involve **VIBRATIONAL FREQUENCIES**, not just energy but different kinds of energy that are often confused by beginners. Once you learn how to tell them apart, you'll be well on your way to a more comfortable and successful life.

You see, the key to playing nicely within today's rules is to *understand* different vibrational frequencies and then *use* them with skill. Once you know how, these skills are easy to master.

Easy, yes. But powerful, too. By contrast, what kind of mess happens when people lack this kind of skill? Millions of us are working really, heroically, hard on ourselves. In ways that don't work. In ways that can't work, not any more.

Well-intended but clueless, instead of flowing with today's rules, so many of us are breaking them. Ironically, millions of people are *suffering more* as a result of all their hard work at self-improvement.

Bring on this **PROGRAM FOR EASY VIBRATIONAL BALANCE**! It was designed to help you adapt to the new rules so that you can thrive.

The program in this book aims to supplement what you're already doing for self-growth... by powerfully waking up your experience of yourself, rebooting your effectiveness at everyday life, and helping you express your soul more fully than ever before.

This newly needed vibrational balance can be achieved pretty easily. You shouldn't have to become a professional energy worker ... or a psychic... or a do-it-yourself psychotherapist... in order to keep yourself functioning well as somebody who lives now. All it takes is knowing what to do differently, and then you follow up. It becomes a habit, making a subtle vibrational shift here or there, gently done.

So Imagine a Life Where....

You're not doing *nothing* to progress in your personal development. Neither are you working way too hard. You're simply leading a balanced life (including your favorite forms of personal growth) and adding an approach that strengthens you vibrationally. Because you understand the basic **RULES** for success, living now.

As for certain energy problems (which you will learn how to recognize), should they come up you will do a little something extra, something designed expressly to solve that particular problem. Let's call these skill sets **TOOLS** for the Age of Awakening.

Rules & tools. Simple, right?

I'll share all this in order to support you as somebody living now, in the Age of Awakening. I invite you to learn what can *really* help to protect your personal energies. It's surprisingly effortless, once you get the hang of it.

Now for Some Down-to-Earth Details

You may have found this book as someone who has *never done energy healing before*. Well, I'll be guiding you through our program as if this entire subject were brand new to you.

By contrast, many of you readers have *plenty of background*, and maybe some baggage, related to what you've been doing already. Long before you found this book, you may have worked hard at energy healing. Or you have background in meditation. Perhaps you entered into awareness of energy through your belief in the mind-body-spirit connection.

Another possibility is that *you've worked on yourself psychologically*. For years. Yet in recent years you have begun to wonder whether there is a missing piece to the psychological puzzle that you've been trying to solve. (And there sure is, a vibrational piece.)

Since 1970 I have worked as a teacher in mind-body-spirit. When I give classes, some students are experienced at working with energy while others are beginners, and plenty more fit somewhere in-between: 50 shades of great.

Happily, one thing I have gained over the years — besides somewhat wrinkly skin — is knowing how to teach people whatever their previous experience. Trust that I can help you at your present level of expertise, honoring you just as you are right now, hard-won wisdom and all. Celebrating that experience, I'll be addressing you here as "**POWERFULLY HUMAN READER**."

This title might not sound like such a big deal, not yet. But by the time you are living The New Strong....

Well, let's put it this way. Your next opportunity for personal growth begins on our very next page.

CHAPTER 2

Your Human Life Is More Than You Think

Before you began this human incarnation, you were still you. Call it being a soul, or a being in a body of light, or how about this? I'm going to call it "Being an angel."

Surely you've heard beautiful things about being an angel. But have you ever wondered, what is the problem with being an angel?

There you were, once upon a time. You lived in a heavenly realm that could be compared to the ultimate gated community. Where you got to stay for free.

Exclusively inhabited by souls with qualities similar to yours, the colors were spectacular — far beyond anything on earth. And just how heavenly was the music? Angelic choirs, celestially Autotuned beyond anything heard on earth!

Altogether it was lovely at your old hangout, your heaven. There were no big problems. You felt totally connected to God and to all that is. As an angel, you could praise the Divine. You could learn. You could serve.

There was only one catch, just one little vexation. *As an angel, you couldn't evolve spiritually.*

Why not? Because that takes friction. Choices. Illusions.

Courageously you selected Earth School as a place to incarnate. It's one of the tougher spiritual academies, yet with such great rewards. Picture a learning planet where...

A soul can incarnate for the purpose of evolving spiritually amid great beauties and, also, intricately complex and compelling illusions.

Your Purpose, Spiritually, While Living on Earth

Have you ever wondered, "What is the purpose of my life?" Well, here's one short answer. The purpose of your life on earth is to evolve spiritually. Service to others may be involved. Or you might find, for certain stretches that you go through, the focus needs to be on fulfilling your own personal needs. Which is honorable too.

Many people expect a way-elaborate version of your LIFE PURPOSE. (Surely you didn't expect the entire meaning of your life to be as simple as the words in a fortune cookie.) Yet extra answers might be *optional* for your spiritual evolution right now compared to that one big idea: the main purpose of your life on earth is to evolve spiritually.

Ironically, one's spiritual evolution can get stuck in a holding pattern while awaiting more specific guidance about purpose. Answers that may never be found!

My advice? (Especially if you have been focused on finding a Sure-Thing, Ultimate, Personal Purpose.) Try this experiment. Accept the simple purpose just mentioned as "Good enough for now."

Because, if you're like many clients I have researched with energetic literacy, it can come as a relief to learn that your spiritual evolution really matters that much. Most of it happens behind the scenes, unbeknownst to your conscious mind. Besides, how fast could you grow, really, if you were constantly checking your evolution in a spiritually self-conscious way?

Powerfully Human Reader, the story of your spiritual progress so far is displayed beautifully in your energy field. During this transitional time, people can evolve especially rapidly, even if the journey has seemed hard. Both psychologically and spiritually, it's likely that you are racing along your personal path. Because we're now living in the Age of Awakening, we can grow faster than ever.

Yes, even when you've felt relatively stuck, you have been evolving fast. What can help you to progress even faster, and consciously know that you're doing it? Align your human life vibrationally. It's simple, once you know how.

More Perspective about Incarnating on Earth

While you were back home on The Other Side, the prospect of this latest incarnation probably seemed much easier than it has turned out to be. Back home, that goal of quick evolution may have felt like a breeze. A romp. Your delightful chance to become an even more glorious angel, closer than ever to God and All That Is.

In theory? A slam dunk. In practice? Trickier.

What is involved in any of these earth adventures, anyway? You leave heaven for a while, take on a body and personality, and adjust to life at the learning planet as best you can. And if you have chosen Earth School, much of your spiritual evolution will boil down to two things:

- **AWARENESS**, a.k.a. consciousness, where the mind directly experiences itself. Awareness also means your ability to notice people and things and energies, living as the unique soul you are.

- **LEARNING**. This can happen quite intensely, depending on who you are this time around.

Learning may come from your health and wealth, social status, family, friends, love relationships, work. Whatever you say and do will generate consequences (a.k.a. **KARMA**), all of which will compound your learning. The same for how you treat people; such as whether or not you choose to help them. At Earth School, the consequences of speech and action become part of your educational experience.

Once a new lifetime begins, choices that you make will either increase the learning or slow it down. Free will is always available. Aiming for happiness might seem like an obvious focus, but it's hardly a soul's only way to learn.

For the sake of your long-term progress, you might choose to slow down your evolution for a while, for instance by prizing a sense of security above all else. Or you might experiment with a dead-end path that doesn't produce what was promised — just so that you can learn "Never again."

Enjoyable or not, every choice that you make will bring consequences. These will produce more learning (probably during that lifetime and, definitely, afterwards). On the Other Side, each freshly completed incarnation will be reviewed for even more perspective on what has been achieved.

"Earth School" — Now That's an Interesting Choice

Planning for your next educational adventure, Earth School was hardly your only option. Given this, perhaps you're grumbling:

Why would I ever want to return to this smelly, violent, super-challenging place?

During depth hypnosis, one of my clients for past-life regression, Mia, described the fascinating job she had as an angel, right before entering into this incarnation.

Before continuing with this teaching tale, here's my disclaimer about names that I will be using throughout this book. They are fictitious. Real-life incidents are reported to the best of my ability. Many students and clients have taught me about vibrational reality, and I want to pass along that wisdom without compromising my professional relationships with them.

Back at Mia, on the Other Side she served as a kind of Incarnational Guidance Counselor. An expert on Earth, as well as several other evolutionary academies, Mia would meet with souls to help them decide where to go next.

"I tell them, 'Earth is a great place to grow fast. But it's not for everyone. Don't underestimate how tough it can be.'"

"Earth isn't for everyone?" Well, folks, too late for you and me to reconsider that choice!

So what if Mia or some other angel warned you in advance? Back in heaven, who fully remembers the pain of their previous lifetimes? Truth is, living on earth as a human will sometimes strain credulity even while we are here. Definitely mess with your concept of "comfortable." And so much more.

Of course, incarnating on earth in a human embodiment also counts as a privilege. To earn that lifetime, I've heard that you must be willing to go through loads of lesser Earth School incarnations. A legendary authority in Hinduism, Swami Brahmananda, taught this: a requirement for incarnating on earth as a human (any human) is for that soul to undergo at least 10,000 lifetimes in other life forms.

Even on a bad day, doesn't your human gig beat living as a mosquito?

And surely you've noticed this, Powerfully Human Reader. Whatever you had to go through to get here, somehow you succeeded in arriving with a head and a heart, plus plenty of other valuable capacities.

Whether you know it or not, being human, you have the chance to *evolve* at a super-challenging place. Maybe not always fun at the time, no Disneyland for the evolving soul. Yet our food? I've heard it's the best in any world.

Most importantly Earth School is an amazing learning academy for the soul. Have you ever considered how much exercise you get by dealing with all of earth's vibrational frequencies?

Those pulsating energies cover an enormous range, whether placed lower or higher.

In music, for instance, the voices in a chorus might range from a deep-voiced bass, through baritone, alto, all the way up to the squeakiest soprano. All these sounds correspond to different energetic frequencies.

Thus, on a daily basis, we humans deal with a huge range of energies. And, did you know? Precious few of them are labeled accurately.

Labeling Earth's Frequencies ACCURATELY

Let's take a little survey of some aspects of earth life that you may not have thought about lately. Why not? Because you have become so well adjusted to your human life.

Okay, stop laughing. I don't necessarily mean that other people would call you "Well adjusted."

No, I just mean that you have learned to pay attention in normalish ways, rather than emphasizing vibrational realities that have no part in everyday, sane, human conversations.

How? Keep reading.

CHAPTER 3

The Clever Little Earth School Conspiracy

Powerfully Human Reader, you have been raised to notice **HUMAN VIBRATIONAL FREQUENCIES** of energy, so let's begin our survey there.

Ever see a baby giggling at "Nothing"? Perhaps little Jaden is waving his hands in the air at "Nothing." As for actually touching some ordinary physical object, wow! That can cause little Jaden to laugh so hard, his wobbly little head nearly falls off.

That miniature human isn't really as goofy as he seems. Jaden is learning to position attention away from angelic-type vibrational frequencies towards what is human. Caregivers consistently train him to prefer human-level objects, like Baby Jaden's physical left foot, not all its dancing lights and wavy energies. No wonder Jaden laughs so much. As if that human-type illusion were one solid object! A thingie. A foot.

Quite the opposite of normal, this "reality" is. Back home in heaven, everyday life was about astral vibrational frequencies. To build a dream house, you just thought about it. Ta-da! Instantly your "creation" would manifest. Your gorgeous new dining table would appear, real as could be — just not fashioned of earthly material. (No shopping needed. And that table wouldn't cost you $5,000 either.)

CELESTIAL, PSYCHIC-LEVEL, ASTRAL: these are synonyms for things made out of energy, rather than physical matter at human vibrational frequencies. Celestial-quality things in your heavenly house didn't seem freaky to you, not once you got used to them. Just as, prior to incarnating on earth, you expected your body to be made of light, rather than human flesh, blood, skin, etc.

Being an angel meant having no human senses to function. Therefore, nothing was real in the physical ways that we humans depend upon, living in a world where energy congeals into so-called "objects" at their crazy-ridiculous, low frequencies. Vibrationally what does "human" mean, anyway?

- ～ Slowed-down energies.
- ～ Dense, heavy energies.
- ～ Energies shaped as solid objects that fit with the rest of physical reality.
- ～ Objective reality that can be measured, counted, captured in digital images, shared.

At human vibrational frequencies, energies are not noticed as such — except for energies that directly affect objective reality, like solar power and wind power. But what about noticing people's vibes? Ha! *That isn't noticing life at human frequencies.* (More on this later.) Back at our human vibrational frequencies, there is also...

Subjective reality: how we feel, what we think; all of which may concern either ourselves or others or both.

Powerfully Human Reader, please note that subjective reality at human frequencies is waaaaaay superficial and dumbed-down. Compared to what? Compared to subjective experiences of *other* frequencies. Living now, adults can readily experience them as well, which is new. (More on this later, too.)

How does baby Jaden relate to human vibrational frequencies? They're new to him. Objective reality is like an exciting puzzle with innumerable moveable pieces. For instance, which objects are solid and won't change a lot — like touching a wooden floor.

Versus other solid objects that change after you do something to them — like sucking a piece of paper until it turns strangely mushy.

Besides that kind of puzzle, what is Jaden to make of liquid objects like water? He watches a caregiver pour this wet thing from one solid pitcher into a sippy cup, yet the pitcher itself doesn't pour? How strange is that?

Animal, vegetable, mineral: so much mystery is packed into every single object at Earth School's slooooooow vibrational frequencies! Our physical objects are complicated, messy, and weirdly beautiful.

Objects that Last? Weirder Still.

Learning about earth vibrationally, young children take a giant step of adjustment once they grasp that physical objects are not only solid but "Permanent." (Sure wasn't like that back home in heaven!)

Let's say that, by this point in his life, Jaden is pretty experienced for a baby. Mom hides a yellow ball from him. Then she shows him that same ball again.

Quite understandably, object permanence might take Jaden months to accept. Every round of "Hide the Toy," Mom's astral energies changed drastically, whether from the fun of the game or else from sheer exhaustion — Mom eventually playing this particular game with Jaden at least 500 times.

With "Hide the Toy," what is Jaden being taught about that ball as an object? It is "real," being assembled from earthly materials, which are strangely solid and about as subtle as a starter box of crayons.

Meanwhile Jaden is being distracted by far more gorgeous astral energies, the kind he's used to noticing. His aura. Mom's aura. All those changes to their personal energies... who wouldn't notice something so obvious? So how can this not be important to Mom?

Jaden knew that a weird kind of dullness was coming. Some preparation was given in heaven; more practice came during womb-time. But really, how unbelievably strange it feels to him now. Seriously, he's supposed to pay rapt attention to these slow-&-clunky, human-level objects?

Not a joke? Not temporary? Aargh!

Instead of living at the speed of thought, Jaden is really expected to settle for those sweetly dopey earth objects. As if they could even begin to compete with what he's used to (and still can perceive all around him), astral energies. These are so much brighter, juicier, and all-around more interesting.

Playing with that yellow ball, Jaden gets it. Nothing seems to thrill Mom except for the most obvious, superficial, Earth-Is-for-Dummies part — how that yellow ball remains a yellow ball. Yeah, right.

Loveable Mom! But seriously, what is wrong with her? Captivated by one corny yellow object.

And no matter how long you play with it, that ball stays exactly the same. What kind of a fool couldn't tell that Mom's energetic changes are way more interesting?

For months, Jaden has found this earth focus impossible to accept. To Mom, "One thingie stays the same" is supposed to be the point of the game, even though all her energies are changing like crazy.

Weird and silly, this game! And yet curiously entertaining at the same time. Object permanence? Duh! Eventually, lesson "learned." The concept was never hard. It's more that Jaden finally gives up and stops resisting the premise of human life on earth.

Congratulations, sorta. Accepting object permanence means that Jaden is better adjusted. He starts finding it easier to aim attention at human vibrational frequencies. Ironically, Jaden seems "smart" because he has agreed to dumb down in the same idiotic way that other humans before him have been required to do.

At the risk of sounding like a Conspiracy Theorist about Vibrational Illusion, I've got to ask you. Powerfully Human Reader, do you realize how much training every child receives on the theme that I've just described here?

Every waking hour, the lessons continue. Every relentless adult teaches the same dumbed-down curriculum: "Only human counts." While energy, glorious energy, is not supposed to matter.

No Wonder Babies Cry So Much

Like baby Jaden, since Day One, you have been programmed to pledge allegiance to human life. Parents *need* to educate/brainwash babies this way. Otherwise they wouldn't progress as "Normal human beings."

To each baby such training may seem like "The survival of the stupidest."

So what? Every well-adjusted child must learn to believe in physical objects as "real," with energy awareness receding. That's just how Earth School works.

Grownups of all kinds, even strangers, offer positive reinforcement whenever a baby acts as though human-vibrational objects are real.

By contrast, what happens if Jaden positions attention at the energies he prefers? (These would be astral energies, plus a bit of Divine glow always tucked into earth life as well.)

Good luck with that, baby Jaden!

What happens if he prefers waving his hands around, touching energies? (Excuse me, in human terms, touching "nothing.")

Negative reinforcement, that's what he'll get. Consistent negative reinforcement from most adults, whether family or neighbors or strangers.

Adding to the indignity, what happens later? Eventually grownup humans will succeed in forcing Jaden to talk. Out loud! Which seems truly ridiculous, at first, to any self-respecting baby.

Ridiculous, why? Since babies speak "Telepathy" just fine, thank you very much. Young children speak it with people, pets, plus any number of astral and Divine presences. Telepathy works great for them, quick as thought and just as effortless.

What's the big exception? Dealing with those intelligence-compromised kids over five. Or those even stranger grownups, who can be crazy-obtuse about communication.

As he grows up, Jaden will practice matching their sound combinations with his real mother tongue, the universal language of Telepathy. Eventually his human-style blabbing will turn fluent. This might seem like a pretty stupid game too, except for the big payoffs.

Because what happens, for instance, when Jaden finally gurgles "Mama"? He gets to watch Mom's aura burst into radiant joy. Plus her physical face turns shiny with happy tears, followed by a very human hug that ripples with extra-big love.

Childhood provides enticements aplenty for Jaden — or you — to focus on earth frequencies. Bit by bit you learn to position attention at there, then speak the required language.

Over the years, Jaden is taught to accept human-level beliefs galore, plus cause-and-effect. He discovers again and again that you never know quite how stupid a human can be until… you find out. So many interesting games are played by grownups!

Kids like Jaden — by which I still mean YOU — are socialized into believing that human experiences are pretty much all that happen on earth. You come to trust objective reality as a kind of one-size-fits-all, dependable basis for life. By adulthood, you may have also been taught (convincingly) that your soul only has one life, ever, and it is happening right now.

After learning so much about how to cope with human reality, you are likely to take it for granted as "all that is." Well, I'm here to remind you, don't. Don't take this for granted.

Juggling Just One Vibrational World? Or Three?

You see, Powerfully Human Reader, unlike the version of truth that you've been taught since childhood, life on earth involves three sets of vibrational frequencies. Not just one, three.

- **HUMAN VIBRATIONAL FREQUENCIES** are central to human experience in any age. (And not including energy awareness, except for kinds of energy that impact physical matter, like calories, temperature, volts.)

- **ASTRAL VIBRATIONAL FREQUENCIES** are the kinds of energy in flower fairies and angels, plus human auras. Reading energies with clarity? That's energetic literacy. Reading energies as a beginner? That's the inexact pastime of "Picking up vibes."

- **THE DIVINE VIBRATIONAL FREQUENCY** is a perfect kind of energy. It is in God, in Jesus and other Ascended Masters; in Archangel Michael and other archangels, and a bit of that is in your own aura as well.

Human, astral, and Divine — you could think of them as three kinds of ball. Growing up we didn't learn how to juggle all three with our attention.

Obviously we learned lots about how to play with one kind, the human-level balls, like that "fascinating" yellow ball in Jaden's infancy. As for the other two kinds of ball, they stayed put right on the floor, as it were. Ignored. Human socialization required playing catch (in awareness) with only one kind of ball, the human-frequency kind.

Now, however, all balls are actively in play at Earth School. So it's time to learn a new skill: *How to safely juggle all three of these very different kinds of vibrational frequency.*

Doesn't that idea seem weird? Mama didn't raise no vibrational juggler. But remember, that was before December 21, 2012.

Now? Powerfully Human Reader, you can definitely learn how to manage today's new attentional juggling. That would be a good idea. Your quality of life depends on it.

For one thing, how else can you follow the new rules for humans on earth? These rules are required if you aim to thrive in this Age of Awakening.

Hey, you probably don't even know about the *old* vibrational rules. So let's explore them next.

CHAPTER 4

Seven OLD Vibrational Rules

All your life you've heard that it's important for people to be "down to earth." This form of praise never goes out of fashion. Think of your favorite politician, athlete, or movie star. Special achievements make them admirable, but sheer humanity is what makes them likeable.

Aren't your favorite celebrities considered humanly relatable? Most of us gravitate towards a person we'd like to have a beer with; folks who willingly roll up their sleeves and get down to work.

Well-adjusted, down-to-earth people used to have such an advantage, given the old vibrational rules. Unspoken rules! These were so obvious, who needed to think about them consciously? Not until those rules changed, anyway.

What exactly were those old vibrational rules? Earth School emphasized human vibrational frequencies, in contrast to frequencies that involve energy. Those subtler experiences used to be really hard to access. A **VEIL**, or **PSYCHIC BARRIER**, kept our awareness firmly grounded in human frequencies.

Yes, even then clear experiences of energy were possible. But seeking that took training and persistence. Or, for some of us, mind-altering drugs. Or — sometimes, mercifully — a mystical experience was obtained through the grace of God.

Historical note: Psychological self-awareness didn't emerge in pop culture until relatively recently, a century or so before 12/21/12. You'll read more about psychological growth starting in Chapter 11.

To sum up, for thousands of years, being human meant noticing human vibrational frequencies. No wonder it was an **AGE OF FAITH**! Beliefs brought comfort, consolation. Somehow life must be more than it seemed. And until deliverance came, keeping the faith would at least bring hope.

With that thick veil blocking direct experience of higher frequencies, what was the best that people could do? Gaze at a stained glass window. Listen to sacred music. Kneel and pray in front of an altar.

Direct experience of the Divine was rare. (Real experience, that is, in contrast to fine-sounding talk.)

Seeking a better life meant clinging to humanly-crafted belief systems, maybe idolizing the best authority figures available. And what else? As a universal kind of consolation prize, people gained steadiness through rules like those you'll read about in this chapter.

For example, when everyday awareness was stuck in human frequencies, how was one to assess whether or not other people were *good*? Human-level appearances, that's how. If a parish priest looked good, that ought to be enough. If he managed to live without scandal, that priest just *had* to be good. He could be trusted.

Think about that idea for a moment. Believing in people because they fit in? When I roll that around in my brain, here's the reaction. "Maybe, it's true, but only up to a point. Besides, what a dangerous way to live!"

What do you think, Powerfully Human Reader? These days, do you trust people simply because they seem to fit in?

Back then, everyday human life was mostly taken at face value. Religion made experiences more digestible, like pepper sprinkled over tough meat. And here's another example of how different life was in the Age of Faith, when awareness was solidly anchored into human vibrational frequencies. Material wealth was often considered synonymous with God's approval.

In this Age of Awakening, we're far less likely to believe that, aren't we? Plenty of other simplistic beliefs are becoming less relevant too, because consciousness can travel so fast and so far, making us way perceptive.

Living without the veil, it's amazing how effortlessly we can plumb a person's inner depths. By contrast, can you remember how difficult it used to be, trying to go deeper within? Even as recently as the 1970's, that was like juggling balls made of concrete. (And if you're too young to personally remember the waning Age of Faith, just ask your parents or grandparents.)

Progressive thinning of the veil began to alter how human consciousness worked. Subtle inner discoveries came faster and faster — a way bigger deal, in my opinion, than outer advances in technology, like personal computing or the Internet or social media. (Don't get me wrong. These *were* a big deal. It's just that our changes related to consciousness were a much bigger deal.)

Granted, our Age of Awakening changes have been subtle. It's unlikely you woke up on December 22, 2012 and thought, "Halleluiah! My consciousness is so much more awake now. Personal growth will no longer be so elusive."

Nonetheless, here we are. Welcome to this Age of Awakening, when human consciousness flows with a new freedom that can make self-actualization more attainable, provided that we know what we're doing. I'm going to teach you how to safely go with the flow, starting with a clear understanding of earth's new vibrational rules.

What Are Vibrational Rules, Anyway?

VIBRATIONAL RULES dictate how to habitually direct attention so that you can succeed in human terms. (Also, following these rules will help with your personal flow of consciousness, how you juggle attention vibrationally.)

You know, living now you have enormous freedom about how you pay attention to yourself and others, a freedom unprecedented in human history. Ironically, relatively few people are making a knowledgeable choice.

Powerfully Human Reader, which type of vibrational experience do you value most as your habitual choice? Have you given that much thought?

With the veil gone, you have freedom that way, and your choices will impact your relationships, your income, even your health. Our vibrational freedom is new in this world. Those of us who make smart choices today will become tomorrow's leaders.

I'm going to help you make informed choices, ones that bring you good results. Once you know about the new vibrational rules, you may find personal growth comes easier. And this knowledge can also protect you from energy adjustment problems, which you would be wise to avoid.

Our next chapters will acquaint you with the new rules and how to follow them. But first things first. In this chapter I'll summarize humanity's vibrational rules during The Age of Faith. Even if you haven't actively considered them before, I have a hunch that you'll find these rules strangely familiar.

I'm especially curious: when you hear these outdated rules, will you find yourself thinking, "Yes, but"?

Let's find out.

Old Rule #1. Do Your Best to Do Your Duty

"Work matters. Social customs must be honored. Well-adjusted people notice what's what and act accordingly."

To your post-postmodern ears does that sound questionable? Well, this is how humans have lived and evolved from time immemorial. From childhood on, you were supposed to do your duty. And no complaining.

Vibrationally, why that emphasis? During one's waking hours, a person would automatically notice objective reality, a.k.a. "human vibrational frequencies." With objective reality defining the scope of life, the status quo was respected. Within that framework, you did your duty and that's what it meant to be good.

Even today, boy scouts take an oath to do their duty. Yet, as the veil thinned, duty has felt increasingly hollow. Personal meaning does not only depend upon fitting in. We've developed a taste for inner life (and not just inner experiences at human frequencies but inner experiences of energy that are *not* at human frequencies).

Given today's new freedom of consciousness, you still can lead a fulfilling life that includes socially-sanctioned right action. Doing right, though — do you agonize over that many times each day? I doubt it. Powerfully Human Reader, can you even remember the last time you thought about doing your duty?

Old Rule #2. Keep Up Appearances

Objective reality used to count for so much more than (human-level) subjective reality. During the Age of Faith, proper behavior was the key to social standing. No matter how badly you felt, you would keep up appearances... unless, tragically, self-respect was completely gone.

- Dressing? That sure wasn't about proclaiming your brand. You dressed properly in accordance with social standards.

- Formality? Keeping a clean home mattered. If possible, you even set aside a pristine parlor for entertaining. (Now you're more likely to invite guests to join you in the kitchen. "The living room is dead" proclaimed the Washington Post in 2015.)

- Sweat? Keeping up appearances used to require considerable physical effort — done, of course, at human vibrational frequencies. For instance, housework took elbow grease.

    Employment? You sure didn't make money by tapping some keys as a knowledge worker in a paperless office. Work meant sweat. Hence the Age of Faith belief, "Success requires 1% inspiration backed up by 99% perspiration."

Sound quaint? Back in the day people believed in hard work and expected it to be rewarded. Today we're aiming for different ways to be special. Hint: They don't necessarily involve human vibrational frequencies.

Old Rule #3. Social Standing Trumps How You Feel

Human relationships used to be highly valued, and not just because they might feel good.

During the Age of Faith, most likely you lived with other people, plenty of them. Daily you had contact with many more. Most likely, farm animals and pets were in your social network, too. (Less than 100 years ago, even city dwellers would see horses on the street; 100 years farther back, herds of pigs roamed New York City and other urban areas.)

Between all your contact with people and animals, a good life demanded getting along with your fellow creatures. To the extent that people sought self-esteem, or a positive sense of self, it was bound up in those human-level contacts.

By contrast, go ahead and ask the people you know, "What gives you self-esteem?" You'll receive answers like, "Jesus loves me" or "My angels show me what to do" or "My therapist says I'm making progress" or "A special person in my life makes me feel good."

Subjective responses are what you'll receive, most likely. Subjective responses that may not involve human-level life at all, but energies. For many of us living now, social standing may not seem terribly important. Really, when was the last time somebody warned you to "Show good breeding"?

Glad to say, you can learn to combine today's needs for self-esteem along with pursuing a respectable social standing.

Old Rule #4. The Best Things in Life Are Human

In the Age of Faith you were encouraged to value the good things of human life. Perhaps you enjoyed the beauty of nature. Maybe you were inspired by cathedrals or other monuments; or paintings, music, books; or the art of conversation. (And I've heard rumors, there has always been sex.)

Back then, you might have believed that all the best things were not only human but free. Although you still might have wished for some shiny, high-status objects! Regardless, the best things in life were... things. Human-level things.

That unseen veil guaranteed that good things and bad were appreciated mostly at a surface level. But hello! Powerfully Human Reader, you no longer live in that Age of Faith. So good luck with being fulfilled by the surface of life alone!

Of course you want more than that. Staying in balance as you seek more? Now that's a clever juggle, and one that I can help you to learn.

Old Rule #5. To Err Is Human. And So Is Responsibility for Solving Problems

Back in the Age of Faith, did people make mistakes? Did problems arise for other reasons, as well? Definitely. But whatever caused problems, human beings were held responsible for fixing them. And that meant deeds, not saying, "I'm sorry I did that, but it's because I'm still working on my issues."

What did it take to solve problems? Saying things and doing things. Or drawing upon your social connections to get help. Perhaps one might seek expert advice from a wise elder. Bottom line: folks were held accountable for straightening things out, which was done in objective reality.

In "Better," a beautiful book of essays by surgeon Atul Gawande, one paragraph could have been written to summarize Old Rule #5:

"We always hope for the easy fix: the one simple change that will erase a problem in a stroke. But few things in life work this way. Instead, success requires making a hundred small steps go right — one after the other, no slipups, no goofs, everyone pitching in."

By contrast, how patient have *you* been lately with assembling a human team, then making a hundred small steps go right?

Think that's just your personal failing? Think again. (And maybe also think, "New vibrational rules.")

Old Rule #6. You Will Be Judged by Your Civility

During the Age of Faith, children were taught manners that were enforced by adults, complete with physical punishment as necessary.

"Behave yourself in public. If you must yawn, cover your mouth. Dress up properly before you go out. Be polite."

Tradition was almost as sacred as religion. And even for the sake of religion, civilized behavior was valued. Good people had to behave appropriately. We were judged on what we did, not our excuses. Yes, civility mattered.

By contrast, what a strange kind of mess constitutes contemporary manners! Paying good money to go see a movie, everyone in the audience will be warned three times or more to turn off mobile phones. Yet many in the theater still can't resist chatting and texting. What's with that?

As we continue to examine life's usually unexamined rules, you may be struck by the connection between today's lack of civility and how old vibrational rules (like #6) have given way to what's new.

Old Rule #7. Spiritual Virtue Means Obeying Your Betters

Obedience… such a sacred word… ha, does it make you start rolling your eyes? And how about believing that certain authority figures count as "Your betters"?

However, when Old Rule #7 was in place, obedience wasn't merely social. Your immortal soul depended upon it. During the Age of Faith, mainstream religion taught people to avoid sin so they could claim victory in heaven. "Your eternal reward" didn't sure mean winning the Lotto and having fun spending your jackpot.

Life was real and life was earnest. Throughout most of human history people *had* to obey authority figures. Disobedience unleashed ugly consequences, whether social or political or spiritual. Besides, who cared what an ordinary person thought or felt? What you wanted didn't matter. Human authority figures were firmly in charge.

Every upright human being was expected to show obedience. How? By doing your duty, keeping up appearances, maintaining social standing. Good character required stewardship of material resources. There were repair shops. (Hey, ever hear of them?)

Even personal relationships weren't primarily about making yourself happy. Instead you were tested, time and again, to fulfill your responsibilities, to solve everyday problems, and to do all of this in a manner that would please authority figures. Thus would you bring honor on yourself and your family.

Honor — how much did that matter? Tellingly Thomas Jefferson concluded the most important document of his time, the Declaration of Independence, by pledging his life, his fortune, and his "sacred honor."

Familiar Yet Strange, Even Creepy

Yes, creepy! That's my personal reaction to all seven of these old vibrational rules. Back in the Age of Faith, there was such emphasis on the surface of life, those nearly inescapable human frequencies. Can you relate to the trapped feeling that often gripped me during childhood? It gave rise to questions like these:

Is that all there is?

Does growing up mean that I will adjust to living in this strange kind of prison?

Will I always feel such an emptiness, such a huge disconnect between what I'm asked to do and what holds meaning for me?

Yet this Baby Boomer had no idea what to do about feeling so trapped, not until well into the 1960s. With each passing decade, I connected more with what felt real to me, the higher vibrational frequencies.

Energy awareness brings a deeper experience to life. My soul hungered for that. Did yours?

Back in the Age of Faith, what could a person do about that yearning for more? Although the veil was thinning more and more rapidly, it remained firmly in place.

Once that veil disappeared forever, Earth School became more hospitable to people like me and, maybe, you. Nonetheless, we still have our share of vibrational rules. And just like the old ones that we've reviewed in this chapter, breaking them won't help us.

What happens to us when we break life's prevailing rules? We suffer.

So let's take the guesswork out of following today's new rules, starting with our next chapter.

Seven NEW Vibrational Rules

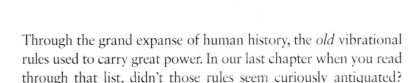

Through the grand expanse of human history, the *old* vibrational rules used to carry great power. In our last chapter when you read through that list, didn't those rules seem curiously antiquated? (Yet familiar.)

Now let's consider the new ones. With the veil gone, everyone can speak the language of energy. So what matters now?

New Rule #1. Choose What Makes You Happy (But Also Remember to Do Your Duty)

In the centuries right before the veil vanished, an idea developed that happiness was an unalienable right. Yet, as this rule reminds us, choosing happiness is no excuse for skimping on human-level obligations.

Why do we even need to be reminded? Now that astral and Divine-level experiences are available to all, "mere" human happiness may no longer seem so appealing.

Back in the Age of Faith, most happiness came exclusively from that more solid version of reality. Besides, how much did happiness even matter? Hence *Old* Rule #1. "Do Your Best to Do Your Duty."

Consider divorce, for instance. A hundred years ago how many in your family got divorced? Quite a simple answer, probably! Because if you married it was your duty to honor that vow.

In the Age of Awakening, many of us divorce. That's because we insist upon happiness and, in general, we're more self-actualizing than our forebears.

Probably you're not used to thinking about vibrational frequencies as a driver of social change. Well, now you can start.

You see, this dynamic of shifting consciousness happens to people all day long, now that the veil is gone. Often the slip-sliding of awareness happens so briefly and spontaneously, it's not going to cause problems. Otherwise? Undue emphasis on astral life won't improve human career or relationships. Instead we're distracted.

Our New Rule #1 acknowledges the central role of happiness in human life, yet cautions us to fulfill everyday obligations. What, it's no longer automatic to reflect upon duty and ethics? That's true. And mostly, I believe, the reason for this oversight is related to humanity's new dynamics of consciousness.

Frequently (and unintentionally), awareness isn't necessarily staying put at human frequencies. In the Age of Awakening, everyday awareness can slip so easily into a higher frequency. So far, most people haven't learned how they can stay in control of this (and, even, attain an easy vibrational balance).

Here's an analogy to help you understand what's happening. Granted, the dynamics being described are very abstract. To help me communicate, I'll invite you to think of a Matroyshka doll, one of those famous nesting dolls.

I've mentioned before that it's possible now to notice reality differently, due to awareness slip-sliding into a higher vibrational frequency. And that, lacking knowledge, we can be clueless when this is happening.

So imagine this. As an example of dealing with physical reality, say that you're playing with your Matroyshka doll. You assume that you're looking at the outermost doll (corresponding to human vibrational frequencies). However, your awareness has slipped into the astral. In terms of consciousness you're actually playing with the third doll inward (that is, perceiving at an astral level).

This higher-vibe reality looks just the same to you. You're looking at "The doll." It feels just the same to you as the big outer doll, even though you're unintentionally playing with that smaller doll.

If you notice any difference at all, it's that you might feel slightly more spiritually awake. In terms of this analogy, there's no clear sign that consciousness is not positioned appropriately, that you're *not* at the level of the outermost doll.

Why would this thought even occur to you? You weren't trying to play with an inner doll. It just happened.

Unfortunately, by playing with that inner doll and not the regular one, you might grow a bit careless about dealing with that outermost level of reality, the human level.

You see, this dynamic of shifting consciousness happens to people all day long, now that the veil is gone. Often the slip-sliding of awareness happens so briefly and spontaneously, it's not going to cause problems. Otherwise? Undue emphasis on astral life won't improve human career or relationships. Instead we're distracted.

New Rule #1 encourages us to stay interested in human life, including that crusty old relic of human vibrational frequencies, about as glamorous as muddy work boots: Doing your duty.

Glamorous or not, this human standard for life can help you grow faster. And you can live this way without returning to the old era's insistence that your personal happiness counts for nothing.

Quite the neat trick! Powerfully Human Reader, this Program for Easy Vibrational Balance is going to teach you how.

New Rule #2. During Your Waking Hours, Emphasize Objective Reality

Under the old rules, even thoughtful people had their awareness stuck at objective reality. Hence the earlier Rule #2, "Keep Up Appearances." By contrast, since the Shift it has become almost automatic to over-emphasize *subjective* reality — and not just the human kind of "subjective."

We're drawn to subjective experience at the subtler frequencies. Adding confusion, we seldom recognize the attentional shift.

Although no longer our automatic focus, *objective* reality still needs to be a priority during a person's waking hours. I'd like to help you renew interest in practical questions like "Who? What? When? Where? How?"

Not just "Why, why, why?"

Powerfully Human Reader, in coming chapters, you'll be shown how enjoyable it can be to follow New Rule #2. Not just to help you win more respect socially but also because it can be so much fun.

New Rule #3. Use Life and Liberty to Pursue HUMAN Happiness

Remember *Old* Rule #3? "Social Standing Trumps How You Feel About Yourself." Really? As if a post-postmodern person like you is about to believe that! We demand happiness, and won't settle for less.

But in the pursuit of happiness, we may often slip-slide into energy awareness and make that our priority. As New Rule #3 cautions us, too much emphasis on inner growth will weaken our progress at Earth School.

Why? To the extent that astral-type personal growth becomes a substitute for human-level happiness, there will be unintended consequences. As in "not pleasant."

Certainly, life grows sweeter when you stop breaking New Rule #3. But why it is broken so often these days? And how can you get back on track (when you didn't even know you were slightly off-track)?

I'll be answering that and providing solutions. Meanwhile please know that, like many of my clients, you will feel much more secure inwardly when you habitually follow Vibrational Rule #3.

New Rule #4. Resist the Temptation to Solve Human Problems Energetically

When push comes to shove, what do you really believe in? With *Old* Rule #4, problems were solved through human means because "The Best Things in Life Are Human."

But in this Age of Awakening, all of us have tasted energies (whether purposely or not), and most of us like that flavor. So, when problems arise, it feels natural for us to reach out and up... towards higher vibrational frequencies.

Hence New Rule #4, which reminds us not to give up on human life, even when tempted to do so.

Since we're mortal, solving human problems continues to demand the human touch. Even when higher vibrational insights can become part of a solution, they won't substitute for saying and doing things in objective reality.

Sadly, many of us have been promised the opposite. We have been told, one way or another, that energies are superior to humble human effort.

Certain energetic shortcuts may tempt us, spiritually or psychologically, for reasons that have plenty to do with this new Age of Awakening.

As you improve your adjustment to human living on earth when the veil is utterly gone (New Rule #4 being part of the deal), you'll find it easier to distinguish what works from what merely sounds good.

Don't be surprised if you develop more patience for solving pesky, human-type problems.

New Rule #5. Stay Invested in Your Human Life, No Matter What

A quality human life demands human-level caring. When you live that way, you're following New Rule #5, which upgrades the older version, "To Err Is Human. And So Is Responsibility for Solving Problems."

With the veil gone, it's so common for awareness to quietly skedaddle into higher vibrational frequencies. Yet we need to keep caring most about our human lives, even if now we can safely do some juggling of higher vibrational frequencies.

Here's an example. Ever hear of TAKING THE SPIRITUAL BYPASS? That means substituting a more alluring energy awareness for doing what it takes to deal with human-type mess. It's today's sanctified equivalent of an old-fashioned, sleazy, get-rich-quick scheme.

And we can do something similar through psychological self-improvement, too, not just religion or spirituality or mysticism. More tempting than ever? Sure. But man oh man, does that ever break New Rule #5! Wouldn't it feel good to follow your chosen path of personal development in a way that works better? I'll be helping you do that.

New Rule #6. Find Human Interest by Interacting Directly with Other Humans

OLD Rule #6 went "You Will Be Judged by Your Civility." Holy cow! Now it's more like other human beings have just moved here from Mars.

And we may only vaguely notice these weirdos… as though *we* weren't one of them.

For example, have you seen folks do this kind of "virtual visiting"? Sitting together with his date at the restaurant, Noah plays with his favorite electronic toys, perhaps texting other friends who interest him more.

Well, behavior like this isn't just rude. It breaks a vibrational rule.

NEW Rule #6 reminds us that *real-time speech and action* are required for quality lives.

Why doesn't texting count? Even when we must use technology often, healthy relationships demand that we also interact regularly in **ENERGETIC REAL TIME.** That means being in a room together, or making vocal contact by phone, or video conferencing live: you plus one or more other human beings.

Accept no substitute, Powerfully Human Reader. Insist upon daily interactions in energetic real time.

For personal growth at Earth School, you need to interact directly and not just electronically. Even a little face time every day can greatly improve your quality of life (and also your vibrational balance).

New Rule #7. Seek Wisely and Humanly, Not Randomly and Astrally

If you weren't already self-actualizing, you wouldn't be reading this book. So lucky you! In this Age of Awakening, earth works better than ever as a mystery school for personal growth.

However, today's curriculum is really, really different. Remember *Old* Rule #7? "Spiritual Virtue Means Obeying Your Betters."

It's more tempting than ever for us idealists to decide for ourselves which authority figures might count as "betters" versus those whose actions deserve a half-hidden eye roll.

Good for us post-postmodern smarties! We decide for ourselves which people to admire, rather than simply doing as we're told. Except it may not be totally wonderful that we're so quick to disrespect those who don't charm us instantly.

Why has it become so easy to do all that sneering and outright ignoring? Are humans really more foolish now than in the days of Shakespeare's "Comedy of Errors" or "The Iliad" or "The Ramayana"?

Hardly. We're just more likely to give a quick sneer, then look elsewhere.

And let's not just blame the Internet or our so-superior irony. We're also distractible due to the (considerable) allure of higher vibrational frequencies.

Yet, with better vibrational balance, we can regain enthusiasm over what earth experience has to offer. Luscious qualities, the kind Shakespeare wrote about: "Shall I compare thee to a summer's day?" Not, "Hey, Baby, I really like your energy."

It can delight you, living in an age when spiritual awakening — the real deal — is available to everyone who seeks it. However, self-actualization demands that we live by the new rules, including Sweet #7.

Harsh life consequences are one way to discover when we have broken this rule, but wouldn't it be great to find a softer alternative? You sure can.

CHAPTER 6

Support of Nature in the Age of Awakening

"Earth's vibrations are rising." Have you heard that idea? Well, it's wrong. Although close. The veil was thinning, and now it's gone. Consequently...

Human awareness is more flexible now. More vibrationally flexible than ever before.

That's the truth. So we can readily access the higher vibrational frequencies, both astral and Divine. (And remember, they're tucked into human-level experience like tiny Matroyshka dolls inside big ones.) If we stop paying attention to human life, we might mistakenly think that astral has become the clever new substitute for human. Except the most important frequencies in this world remain human.

As you learned from exploring today's new rules versus the old, despite our new vibrational freedom, it's still not smart to neglect human life.

No matter what your path of personal development, it's wiser to follow today's new vibrational rules. Becoming. Better. Adjusted. As. A. Human. Who. Lives. NOW.

That, of course, is one requirement to live The New Strong. I'll help you find a comfortable way to follow today's rules. As a result, you'll receive more support of nature.

Yes, You Can Gain Full Support of Nature

But what does that even mean, SUPPORT OF NATURE? Although many of us have never heard the expression, all of us can benefit from this powerful resource. Laws of nature make Earth School run. Obeying natural law makes your life easier, while lawbreaking brings problems.

Sure you *can* fight city hall, but it's smarter to choose your battles. For example:

- To maintain your human body, you have been given a circulatory system, respiratory system, digestive system, and so forth. Each of these systems is supported by laws of nature. If you eat what agrees with your digestive system, you'll be following biological laws of nature.

- To maintain your place in society, you have been taught certain manners and customs. Some people care about them a lot. Others don't. Regardless, you stand to gain socially by using the best manners you can afford. (And here you can definitely afford the very best.) Following social laws of nature gives you "class" and can help you earn more money.

- About your financial standing, think about where you live now. Do people usually barter for beads? By using society's legal tender, there's less haggling, more purchasing power, and no life behind bars. That's following financial laws of nature.

In short, every aspect of your life includes certain laws of nature. When following them, you receive an underlying energetic assist, a.k.a. the *support* of nature.

WHERE *you live* means that certain natural laws apply. When the Alaskan winter comes you'd better dress warm, right? Otherwise you might pay a price, and not just a few odd looks.

WHEN *you live* matters too. Whatever your social class happens to be, don't expect great results by challenging anyone to a duel.

That went out of fashion years ago, drastically out of fashion. If you insist on dueling now, you just might wind up in a psych ward.

For behavior that's considered normal, like appropriate clothing or polished manners, fashions change. Yet, there have always been laws of nature. And there always will be.

In post-postmodern society, we enjoy a flexibility that is unprecedented. Yet still not unlimited. What if you don't happen to believe in the law of nature called "gravity"? Would that make it smart to leap from a rooftop? As police officers say, "Ignorance of the law is no excuse."

Subtle Shifts, Real Consequences

Life on earth has always involved laws of nature. Now some of those laws work differently, and we're the first people on earth to deal with them. After we moved into the Age of Awakening, how many of us knew where to look for change? Only now are we starting to *bear witness*, to understand what has happened and then take advantage of the excellent opportunities before us.

Admittedly, those opportunities — like the new rules themselves — are subtle in nature. Certain opportunities that you'd be wise to choose... concern vibrational frequencies, and it takes a certain inner awakeness to even be interested. I'm very glad that you are, Powerfully Human Reader.

Living now, your opportunities for self-actualization are unprecedented. In this Age of Awakening, millions of people can move into Enlightenment. And do it as householders, not renunciates.

At least, that's how I view the potential before us... because my life work has made me passionate about this thing called "Enlightenment." Whichever words *you* have been using for your highest ideals about personal growth, precisely *that* is attainable now.

And why? Simply because you live now. Plus you're going to learn how to play by today's new rules. You can muster up your pioneering spirit and help lead humanity.

Be among the first to actively use support of nature, as it works now, to fulfill your dreams of personal evolution. Use your full potential in life? Yes, you can make that come true. Self-actualization is a realistic potential for us now, living in the Age of Awakening.

Sadly, ever since the Shift, there have been big new problems. Some of these have occurred because humanity received no memo about new rules in the Age of Awakening, not even news crawl at the bottom of our busy TV screens.

How many of us noticed all the energy talk? Even fewer have realized the vibrational significance of what has been happening, or understood how to gain support of nature under today's new rules.

When it comes to those unheralded vibrational changes, most of us have had to figure things out for ourselves. Many of us have been learning the hard way, breaking the new rules until we felt unbelievably frustrated. At least this has led us to seek a solution.

Breaking today's vibrational rules — can that really cause struggle and suffering? Definitely. And these are very human kinds of suffering, not necessarily feeling "high-vibe" at all. Well, no repining! Improvement starts now.

To be specific, right now you're completing Part One of this Program for Easy Vibrational Balance. It's a good start, knowing about those seven new rules. But this doesn't mean you know enough to make a practical difference, not yet.

Let's continue with our program. I want to help you benefit fully from the new energetic setup on earth. Consider this a definite can do!

Today's Well-Adjusted Human, SPIRITUALLY

Now that we have had The Talk about Today's Vibrational Rules in the Age of Awakening, maybe it has occurred to you. Unintentionally you may have been taking a few little vibrational risks. And then those risky behaviors caused problems that you *did* notice.

Part Two will help you to consciously understand how vibrational rule-breaking can cause plenty of human-type problems.

For now, just know that you're hardly alone. You're not only living in the Age of Awakening: These are the transitional years, unprecedented on the planet.

Unlike generations to come, we're not *vibrational* natives of this age, taking the new energetic arrangement in stride. By way of comparison, think of today's *digital* natives. Their comfort with technology amazes Baby Boomers like me. But for them, it's natural to know their way around iAnything.

Similarly, adjusting to the Age of Awakening can be tough if you were born before the Shift clicked into place. You have every right to feel a bit sorry for yourself. Caught in this transition, life on earth has become an unpredictable, super-complicated, crazy-making challenge… including what happens to us on a daily basis concerning subtle shifts of consciousness.

What about all the scientific research that we depend upon to keep ourselves safe? Psychologists and neuroscientists and others can help explain our lives to us; when they hit the nail on the head, it is so reassuring.

Only they haven't even found the right nail to hit — this not-shiny, super-abstract nail about how human consciousness functions now in some entirely new ways that include an unprecedented vibrational freedom.

With all due respect, scientific knowledge today isn't any more help than mainstream culture or the media. I applaud you for somehow finding this pioneering Program for Easy Vibrational Balance.

Yes, you can avoid mistakes that millions of people around you are making at this transitional time. These mistakes are perfectly understandable, caused by breaking subtle vibrational rules that our politicians can't legislate any more than today's scientists can measure.

Even some of the smartest people are making mistakes, resulting in consequences that involve enormous suffering. Although common today, such mistakes don't have to mess up *your* life.

Every human being can become well-adjusted to this Age of Awakening. Maybe you'll even take a leadership role, bringing clarity to friends who are working so hard while unintentionally breaking today's rules.

Definitely *you* can learn to play nicely within these new rules. Then energetic momentum will be on your side, so you can progress faster than ever before, dancing along your chosen path of personal growth.

CHAPTER 7

Energy as a Most Alluring New Toy

Being human, you'll strengthen yourself vibrationally by committing to human life. Obvious by now, right? Relishing the moment and savoring life's juicy details, how simple that sounds! Not constantly trying to dress up everyday life with energy awareness or working on yourself psychologically. Of course, that ought to seem preferable.

Except that, vibrationally, maybe that preference isn't so automatic. Not any more. In our Age of Awakening, with the metaphysical veil utterly gone, it has become all too common for everyday awareness to slip-slide away from human vibrational frequencies... into astral-level frequencies. Then, suddenly, we may feel oh-so-perceptive and wise.

In this new Age of Awakening, could energy have become your shiny new toy?

- To be fair, energy awareness has become almost everybody's new toy.
- Although astral, it feels *spiritual*. What a thrilling toy if, for instance, after years of unanswered prayers, now you can believe you've gained instant access to God (or God's messengers).
- For some, the preferred plaything has become astral-level experience with a *psychological* spin.
- While other folks combine interest in both toys: a diving toy for psychological insight and also a reaching toy for a new sense of spiritual connection.

↝ Still others proudly scoff at noticing anything fancier than human-level life, disbelieving in anything else. This could be considered a triumph of the socialization process you read about in Part One. (This could also be called "**SPIRITUAL SHUTDOWN**," a way to be thoroughly stuck spiritually, prizing security above all else and, inadvertently, slowing down personal growth.)

Here's an example of somebody who began slipping into energy awareness, then got so hooked that now he plays with it on purpose. A lot!

Aiden's Secret, His New Pride and Joy

This teaching tale is drawn from a conversation that I had with Aiden one sunny afternoon in 2015. There we were, chatting at a Starbucks, enjoying some face time. Smiling, Aiden started to tell me about his latest interest, how he loves to read people's energies.

↝ As he described some of those insights, I began to cringe. Why?

↝ Aiden's observations of energy were pretty basic, suggesting the beginner's stage of energetic literacy.

↝ Yet Aiden didn't know enough to tell how basic his insights really were. He was quite taken with these energy-flavored insights, as if he was learning "Everything. The real truth."

↝ Evidently a lifestyle was developing for Aiden; he was dipping in and out of energies all day long.

Yes, Aiden was responding like billions of people on earth, now that the veil has gone. It has become super-natural for him to dip in and out of energy awareness.

Energy awareness is one of our shiny new toys in the Age of Awakening. Just because it has stopped being difficult to notice astral frequencies, does that mean we have developed energy *skills*? Hardly!

Aiden, for instance, had no idea what he was doing. Nor did it occur to him that skills might even be relevant. He was simply infatuated with all his random experiences. At this point in our conversation, I had a choice to make. Bear in mind, Aiden knew nothing about my work with energy skills. We were just auditioning each other as possible friends.

As he continued regaling me with his energy experiences, Aiden clearly expected praise. Soon I had to make a choice. Was I going to step into my role as a professional at energetic literacy? Or would it be better to smile back at him and nod approval. Clearly Aiden expected me to say something like "Oh, how special you are!"

In this case, I decided to offer education. That's something I seldom do these days in my social life, not with neighbors or folks at the gym, etc. Still, I wasn't the one who had introduced the topic and wouldn't let it go. So I made that decision, even if it might squash my (increasingly unlikely) new friendship with Aiden.

Aiming for maximum tact, I said, "Because of the work that I do, I have a perspective on what you were saying, Aiden. Would you like me to share it, or shall we talk about something else?"

After Aiden agreed to the share, I explained a bit about energetic literacy. He was off to a good beginning with that, I said, yet he could do even better. "Aiden, some people learn skills to supplement their talent for reading energies. If you do that, you can gain loads more information, so what you learn can improve your life even more."

Sadly that squished my friendship with Aiden, squashed it like a bug. Eventually he may remember this conversation and reconsider his energy infatuation.

Meanwhile you're way ahead of him, Powerfully Human Reader. You're willing to learn from this energy skills teacher. Other folks you know might be like Aiden and care more about their pride.

They feel oh-so-special due to noticing energy, which makes them far too gifted to need a teacher. (They think.) Understandable, though unfortunate.

Reading Energies Today Is Like Discovering Sex

Puberty, remember that? Back then, special new feelings would stir within you. Sexual energy was awakening, and wow!

For teens, sex becomes the shiny new toy. Woe to the grownup who says, "Sex is great, thrilling, sacred. Watch out, though, because there are important things to learn about sex that you don't necessarily know."

Which skills might a teenager learn about sex? Skills that don't seem quite relevant to exploring the new thrills:

- How to prevent pregnancy.
- Why, even when hormones are screaming for sexual exploration, it still would be wise to take things slowly.
- Which behaviors show respect for your sexiness and which don't. (Please, kids, no midnight booty calls.)
- And how to avoid getting hurt.

True, each person's sexual energy is inherently beautiful, and sexiness could even be considered a kind of talent. For happiness, though, talent alone won't suffice. Bring on appropriate knowledge and skills!

Well, the same goes for reading energies. Veil gone equals effortless access, but neither knowledge nor skills is necessarily part of the equation. We risk too much energy reading, energy talking, energy healing. A little is fine. Too much causes problems.

No longer are we living in the Age of Faith, when awareness defaulted to human frequencies. Now it's so tempting to favor what's astral over the merely human, going overboard on flashy experiences.

Like Aiden, you'd feel special doing this, too. Only later would you notice some pretty undesirable consequences, including the kind of lifestyle problem you'll learn about in a couple of chapters.

Vibrational Skills Can Protect You Enormously

In reality, it's naive to play with energies just because you can. For one thing, many newbies to energy awareness know so little about it, they think it's plenty to sort their experiences into "good energy" and "bad energy." This unskilled approach leads to self-protection practices that can waste a lot of time.

By contrast, skilled energy healers know that many different kinds of astral-level energies exist, causing different problems if they get stuck in the human energy field. Effective energy healing requires training, discernment, and a range of skills.

For example, in RES we have identified 15 different kinds of STUFF. Each is a specific type of astral-level garbage that can lodge within a person's aura. (In Part Four of this book you'll learn skills for prevention and permanent healing of some of these kinds of STUFF.)

Seems to me, both energy *reading* skills and energy *healing* skills are required to do more than talk a good game. Lacking skill, theories arise that sound appealing but simply aren't true. Popular examples are fearing:

- Energy vampires
- Psychic vampires
- Toxic personalities

Do millions of people fear these? Sure. But do these scary creatures really exist? Nope. (Which you can verify for yourself after you have developed solid skills for energetic literacy.)

Granted, those 15 other kinds of STUFF really exist, just not the much-dreaded vampires. Every year I'll do more than a thousand sessions, helping clients to remove STUFF permanently. Neither I nor the professionals I've trained have ever encountered a single problem that was caused by an "energy vampire."

So why are these scary forms of "bad energy" so well known? With all respect, the fear mongers are only beginners at energetic literacy. They do notice something real, only discernment is lacking. Had they better skills, the storied vampires wouldn't be blamed.

Of course, anyone's imagination can run riot when prompted by fear. For instance, what if some author on Hay House radio were to warn you that the biggest cause of "bad energy" was neon-green energy potatoes? Not so hard to picture (even though they don't really exist). You might begin spotting those potatoes in the energies of folks you dislike, especially if you believed that playing "Find the Evil Potato" would protect you.

Vanquish the fear of energy vampires? Sure, you can do that on your way to The New Strong. In later chapters you'll learn dependable skills for energy healing, using techniques that have been tested internationally. I'm also going to teach you how to *prevent* problems related to energy. That protection begins with consumer smarts about human vibrational frequencies versus the astral ones.

Living in this Age of Awakening, we can't afford to take our humanity for granted. And yet, as you'll learn in the next chapter, many people have fallen into a pattern that inadvertently disrespects the gift of human consciousness.

CHAPTER 8

The Enticing Romance of the Astral

At this point in our Program for Easy Vibrational Balance it's time for a warning about THE ROMANCE OF THE ASTRAL. This means preferring astral vibrational frequencies to what is "merely" human.

Just what's so alluring about the astral? Glamour. By contrast, our wacky world is dense-intense. Purposely designed that way, actually. Making progress at your job, for instance, requires more than a wish. As for finishing a seemingly minor chore? Well, the tiniest home repair can require four trips to Home Depot.

Grrrrrr! Have you ever wondered why trivial things can take so much time? Maybe you can relate to Rose Rosetree's LAW OF STUPID CHORES: *The stupider a chore, the longer it takes.*

Like it or not, that's Earth School. The place is designed for spiritual evolution, not an endless succession of giggles. Even after the Shift, our learning academy runs vibrationally at distinctively heavy frequencies, good old human vibrations. Seemingly meaningless chores take loads of time, and probably always will (no matter what new technology promises).

Why does this have to be? Earth School is meant to challenge us. Given frustration, will we crumble? Can we muster the strength to face our problems and solve them? Every day we must choose whether to score a new point in the game of life... or to miss that chance.

What about this game changes with the new vibrational rules? Now we must *make the choice* to commit to human reality. Otherwise we'll often space out, drifting into an astral experience that might automatically seem sweeter, wiser, more exciting, and far more glamourous. Only we're breaking those rules.

But what kind of glamour exactly? Within the range of astral frequencies, there are loads of possibilities. Each brings its own quality of astral dazzle:

- **LOW-ASTRAL GLAMOUR** is like beer commercials. You're given a pleasantly tipsy version of life: Feeling sexually desirable, mellow, and wonderfully popular.

- **MID-ASTRAL GLAMOUR** is like when your friend Claire brags that "Spirit guides just found me another parking space." The pleasing paranormal buzz could feel like being high on marijuana. Highlights include a sense of belonging to an in-group that's spiritually superior.

- **HIGH-ASTRAL GLAMOUR** is like the very trippy effects of heroin or cocaine. When it's a good, clear high, consciousness flows in a way that can make us feel we're oh-so-close to God's golden glow. Not that the experience really is vibrationally Divine. No, we just lift up achingly close... before we come crashing back down to earth.

What do all astral-level experiences have in common? They're perfumed with more glamour than anything human. Even true of experiences at the lowest astral frequencies!

And what else is tricky? Any experience at an astral level can be mistaken for something recognizably human, although really it's different. You know, like one of the smaller Matroyshka dolls.

Depending on where your consciousness is positioned, you could be having an astral-level experience even though you assume that awareness is right on the surface. It's easy to lose touch with human objective reality and be charmed by subtler versions of experience that are more intense and seductive. Potentially addictive, too — as flashy as the fabled casinos of Las Vegas, only more so. Hence another term I like to use for that glamour, "**ASTRAL FLASH.**"

A habit can develop where a person finds human frequencies boring and, instead, lives in thrall to the astral. Throughout human history certain people have had that problem, opium addicts for instance. But as a way of life... for *millions* of people... to prefer astral flash? And without taking recreational substances? Now that's new.

However, this happens to be a very common adjustment problem in this new Age of Awakening.

But how does this drugless high happen, exactly? I could give examples from Evangelical Christianity or Zen Buddhism or other religions. Instead, here's an example from New Age Spirituality, regarding a New Age pursuit that has gone mainstream.

Seeking Advice from Spirit Guides

Here is how to solve all your problems (supposedly). "Close your eyes. Look within. Find your spirit guide. Ask for advice, because this beautiful angel is your personal Messenger of God."

Or maybe you have purchased a deck of angel cards and been told something like this, "When you choose a card at random, that means synchronicity, like receiving God's tap on your shoulder. Archangel Michael (or whoever) is waiting to help you."

Then we're invited to surrender to the comfortable astral feeling. "Ask for the solution to any problem. It will be solved. As a bonus, the process of listening to angelic messages makes you more spiritual." Supposedly.

Man oh man! The veil disappears and millions of smart spiritual seekers can get pretty confused for a while. Sure it's fun to seek guidance from so-called "higher beings." But how helpful is that really? Why seek that when you're an entirely different kind of being, the kind called "human"?

Who Are These Spirit Guides, Anyway?

You came to earth with a **PERSONAL ANGEL TEAM**, Divinely authorized to assist you. At birth, your team included a guardian angel plus a couple of spirit guides. Over time, additional guides and angels may have been added, all of them also Divinely authorized.

Picture these astral helpers like members of your sports team, each one wearing a matching t-shirt with your soul's logo. It's a support job. Your Personal Angel Team exists for that purpose, support.

Your authorized angels stay in the background. That way you can be in charge of your life. Should you start to seriously lose your way, or an emergency arises, advice will be whispered into your subconscious mind. In a big emergency, that advice will be screamed.

For example, here's a teaching tale from my client Annabelle.

When Annabelle's Angels HAD to Speak up

The housewife was being attacked by her abusive husband. He had hit her before. Only this time it felt scarier, like he meant to kill her.

Suddenly Annabelle heard a loud voice inside her ear, "Right in back of you, on the bureau, there's a big bowl. Pick it up NOW and hit him on the side of the head!!!!!!!!!!"

Annabelle did that. It saved her life. After knocking out her abusive husband, she left him. Finally.

Since then, Annabelle has moved forward just fine on her human path. No longer do angels need to scream in her ear. That life-saving incident was a one-time exception to the usual work of Annabelle's Personal Angel Team.

Powerfully Human Reader, I hope that your personal team will never need to intervene in such a manner.

What is a healthy way to have an ongoing relationship with your Personal Angel Team? They're lovely, so thank them once a day, if you like.

Otherwise, please don't pester them. Too much contact would only distract you from your main job at Earth School, which is *evolving as a human being*. That includes making your own choices in life.

What's Wrong with Asking Angels for Help?

Consulting with angels and saints has been done for centuries. But since the Age of Faith ended, too much guidance-seeking can cause problems. Begged for advice all day long, a member of your Personal Angel Team might be tempted to quit the regular job and become an advisor instead. All of us want to be important, right? That goes for astral beings too. Angels and guides, even venerated saints, can be corrupted. Just like us humans.

Kira Heston, one of my students, used to belong to a psychic development group that was dominated by enthusiastic bragging about work with spirit guides. One time Kira asked her main guide, "Am I working enough with all of you? I know I'm not spending much time at all." He reassured her, "That's just fine."

Usually, though, who will respond to questions like that? Nobody from your Personal Angel Team. And not the saint you learned about in Catholic school, either. Who, then?

Spirits aplenty lurk around you right now. Earth has always had ghosts; since the Shift their number has increased dramatically. Many of these random spirits are eager to be promoted to so-called "Spirit guide."

If you give one a chance to advise you, what will happen? Expect to receive "wondrous" insights on all matters great and small. Many beautiful spiritual seekers become dependent, pleading for guidance all day long. This can become addictive. (Until you decide to stop. Which, of course, you can.)

Something similar happens these days in business. To increase profit, some American executives choose to outsource jobs to foreign workers. Well, human beings can outsource too, putting astral spirits in charge of their human lives.

Tempting, in this Age of Awakening! Unless you know better. Folks, we came to earth to evolve. Adults do that by making choices for ourselves. Obedience training is for dogs, not people.

Another Reason to Avoid Outsourcing to Spirit Guides

Astral beings are no more connected to God than you are. Your direct connection to the Divine is already magnificent, sturdy and powerful, perfect for somebody who has incarnated as human.

Although astral entities are also connected to God, their access is no better than yours. Especially an *astral* being who is so confused or corrupt that it presumes to advise *human* beings, as if giving orders from on high. ("On higher," anyway. "High" means Divine. Astral means "Higher.")

Consulting with non-human beings will not make you a privileged character, free from the limits of other mortals. No amount of trust in angels can successfully outsource human responsibilities, like paying attention to objective reality and doing those gnarly but necessary — often stupid and time-sucking — chores.

Yet in some circles, random astral entities are sometimes confused with Divine-level beings, as if it's the most natural thing in the world for Jesus to tell you what to buy at the health food store.

Truth is, Divine Beings don't advise humans on routine shopping purchases. Bossy spirits do. (Of course, we humans can also shop on our own. Last time you checked, didn't those stores exist on earth?)

A variation on guidance seeking is using a pendulum, whose movements are interpreted as signifying a cosmic "Yes" or "No."

Supposedly it makes sense that valuable guidance comes that way. As if you're some lowly life form who can receive proper knowledge only when using a simple trinket that dangles from a chain?

Ridiculous! Almighty God doesn't need to work through a pendulum. And don't be so sure your Higher Self is moving that thing, either. More likely it is controlled by a ghost or some other discarnate entity. Truth is, an unscrupulous astral being could be having great fun making you dance.

Sometimes it reminds me of the bygone Age of Faith, how fervently some of today's spiritual seekers depend on angels. Ethan, for instance, never even considers that the "Guardian Angel" who gives him guidance could be lying. Look, that's as naive as assuming that humans never lie or get delusions of grandeur. If you visit the nearest mental hospital, guess what? You can meet plenty of inmates who will tell you their name is "Jesus." Does that qualify them to advise you?

And Ethan isn't the only human who blindly trusts any advice that seems to come from "The Other Side." As though that meant "of God."

Of course it doesn't. God doesn't micromanage human beings. When life is tough, we may long for answers that require only simple surrender. But that's a fantasy. Reminds me of the beloved movie, "The Wizard of Oz." Wouldn't human life be so much easier if we could just "Follow the yellow brick road"?

Hey, think about that movie for a moment. Just about everything in the land of Oz is bright green. And there's only one road in the entire place. And this road happens to be bright yellow. (Just in case finding it would be too hard otherwise?)

Sure, from childhood on, we humans have moments when life does seem too hard to bear. That's a great time to go watch a movie, not time to get hooked on The Romance of the Astral. What's wrong with this?

- ⌒ Every day, countless times, Ethan checks with his spirit guide.
- ⌒ He tries really hard to be a clear channel for the "wisdom."
- ⌒ Ethan strives for obedience, true spiritual surrender.

Hello, how does this differ from *worshipping* that astral being?

Ethan may not have computed that consciously. But in every other respect, Ethan is worshipping his so-called "spirit guide" — an astral being who isn't even willing to tell the truth about who he is.

A Smarter Way to Seek Advice

Whether it's begging for guidance from astral spirits or exploring energy *anything* all day long, The Romance of the Astral slows down personal growth.

Ironic but true, far from being a shortcut to success, astral flash distracts us. Olivia, for instance, lives as though every decision she makes is a test of spiritual obedience. What if she were to stop checking with her "so-spiritual" — but really astral — guide? Imagine, Olivia making her own decisions!

What would happen, actually? Immediately Olivia's choices could become informative. That way, no matter what, she would win. Not only would she strengthen herself vibrationally but Olivia could learn from the consequences of her actions. Potentially that's huge personal growth, plus cumulative effectiveness and wisdom.

Courage is required to function as your own (human) person. But what's the alternative, really?

Flirting with The Romance of the Astral, though understandable, breaks today's rules. When you emphasize human input instead, you're honoring those rules. And human life will reward you accordingly.

CHAPTER 9

Choose a Smart Consciousness Lifestyle

Can a person really find astral awareness so charming, it becomes a substitute for valuing human life? Unfortunately, yes. Either through spiritual practices or working on themselves psychologically, or both, millions of people are stuck that way.

Without knowing it.

(Maybe even you.)

Of course, anyone can get un-stuck. Because we can choose how to position our consciousness. What does that mean, **POSITIONING CONSCIOUSNESS?** Whenever awake, you aim your consciousness at one vibrational frequency or another. Whichever patterns develop become a "**CONSCIOUSNESS LIFESTYLE.**"

For example, **SPIRITUAL ADDICTION** happens when human life is routinely disregarded… in favor of noticing energy. Which means routinely positioning consciousness at astral-level vibrational frequencies.

With the veil gone, we can slip into that so comfortably now. Comfortable or not, over-dependence on astral life breaks the rules of our new Age of Awakening, where the astral can either support our human lives or distract us.

You see, personal growth today depends on our habits for positioning consciousness. Awareness has become very fluid compared to before the Shift. Astral-level experiences can become a kind of substitute for human engagement. Ironically, this happens even if we're aiming for self-knowledge. Despite our sweet aspirations, whenever we break life's vibrational rules, we slow our progress.

Spiritual addiction can creep up on people, just as smoking an occasional joint might lead to a daily habit. A habit that other folks call "Being a pothead."

Except spiritual addiction requires no chemical assist. It's simply a lifestyle choice that wasn't labeled correctly. Do any of these examples remind you of people you know?

- Grace cares a lot about personal development. One New Age helper after another has coached her to find her path. By now, she feels very close to finding her sacred purpose. Constantly looking for signs and synchronicities, "She is making huge progress in her spiritual evolution." (She thinks.)

- Gemma has learned to trust in her guides. A pendulum is her preferred way to communicate. And does that pendulum ever get a workout! Gemma feels as though she has learned the secret of self-realization, plus everything else she might ever desire. "Just request angelic guidance, then obey. A sacred life is that simple." (She thinks.)

- Glen meditates every morning. Every night, too. In between he strives for detachment, trying for Enlightenment by acting like Mr. Mellow. "Perfecting myself energetically is the true meaning of life." (He thinks.)

- George has been told that spirituality means being positive, so he works on that constantly. Special crystals help, plus aromatherapy, plus healing techniques and, most of all, the power of his fiercely positive attitude. In one day, George might fix his negative thoughts 500 times. It's worthwhile, because "Eventually I won't have any more of those weak thoughts." (He thinks.)

What do all these sweet, striving people have in common? Each one works hard in a way that breaks the rules of this Age of Awakening.

How Spiritual Development Practices Can Break Today's Rules

Let's take another look at these four dedicated seekers. Each one is breaking today's new vibrational rules with spiritual practices that sound beautiful. But vibrationally what's happening?

- When Grace seeks her meaningful coincidences, she sweetly interprets them as "God's way of remaining anonymous." Where does this position her consciousness, toward Divine vibrational frequencies? Nope. Away from human reality and into the astral. Before the Age of Awakening, Grace would just have been distracting herself. Now? Her awareness is chronically positioned at a psychic level. She lives in spiritual addiction.

- Gemma forgets that God gave her a brain and a heart; good judgment and common sense. Sure, by substituting her pendulum, all choices have been simplified. But mostly that's because she's ignoring real life while playing around with spiritual addiction.

- While meditating, Glen might have awareness positioned at Divine frequencies. Might not. Depends on what he *does* while meditating. No question, though, where his awareness goes while practicing detachment outside of meditation: Breakfast at the astral. Lunch at the astral. Dinner at the astral. Snacking at the astral. Yes, it's ironic that Glen's love of God is taking him away from Divine frequencies and also distancing him from human life. He's working so hard, and for what? Right now he's living in spiritual addiction.

- As for George's attempts to be positive... You guessed it. He has found another way to move into spiritual addiction. Incidentally, those pesky human emotions will never go away. They're human. True, lulling himself into spiritual addiction can soften the impact of negative emotions. So would a long nap.

Four Consciousness Lifestyles, Your Choice

A beautiful yearning drives these four good people. (And maybe drives you, too.) Well, there's a way to satisfy that yearning with results that are helpful, not harmful. Powerfully Human Reader, you can purposely choose a smart CONSCIOUSNESS LIFESTYLE.

Lifestyle means a way that you habitually live. Either you can choose it purposely or you might fall into it as a kind of "Whatever. What do I care?" For example, you don't just have a consciousness lifestyle. You have an exercise lifestyle. Among many possibilities, can you relate to any of the following exercise lifestyles?

- Avid runner.
- Using a smart watch to keep fit.
- Lifting weights three times a week.
- Couch potato.

That last one, not actively chosen, still amounts to a choice. And there will be consequences. In this Age of Awakening I have noticed four very popular consciousness lifestyles. Three of them break today's rules, but the fourth can really accelerate personal growth.

1. Spiritual shutdown

Just because the veil is gone, does everyone value our newfound vibrational freedom? Definitely not. To some, it can feel downright dangerous.

Spiritual shutdown is a consciousness lifestyle defined by resistance to energy sensitivity. Although that sensitivity comes naturally now, it can still be squelched. Many folks do just that, proudly avoiding any conscious experience that goes deeper than the surface level of human life.

Security is emphasized, rather than personal growth. Comfort is reinforced by fear of change. Here's one example: "Give me that old-time religion. And it's good enough for me."

There can be considerable suspicion of people who do things differently, even a feeling of being under attack and outnumbered by strangers who are dangerously "wrong."

In the spiritual shutdown lifestyle, a person resists anything energetic or spiritual. Or psychological. (As if "Psychological growth is only for people who are either crazy or weak.")

Preferences like these don't just impact surface-level values and behavior. Energetically what develops? An aura-level inflexibility, with habitual guardedness towards higher vibrational frequencies.

Stuck in this consciousness lifestyle a person may develop increasingly rigid opinions, self-righteous beliefs, and strongly-justified prejudices. Ironically this lifestyle is perfectly compatible with being religious. My research with energetic literacy has shown that the majority of fundamentalists (in any religion) are living in spiritual shutdown.

Millions of people on earth are living this way now, so there's plenty of company. Energetically, though, there's always a price to pay. A type of energetic STUFF, **GRAY SLIME**, is often deposited in the auras of people who live in spiritual shutdown. This results from resistance to the fluid consciousness of the Age of Awakening. So literally, as well as figuratively, spiritual shutdown is a way of being energetically stuck.

Of course, this astral-level STUFF can always be healed. First, though, a person must begin to pursue a different consciousness lifestyle. Later in this chapter I'll explain how.

2. Spiritual addiction

In spiritual addiction, astral energies are over-emphasized, while human vibrational frequencies are considered inferior. A common belief goes, "If only I become spiritual enough, all my (human) problems will be solved." An example is trying to become more spiritual by asking "What would God have me do?" and then trying to live up to that standard. Many spiritual paths encourage the equivalent.

Another example: Many New Age practices have gone mainstream, and they lead to spiritual addiction... now. During the years preceding the Age of Awakening, things were different. For many of us it was important to get involved in energy talk. We blossomed by experimenting with guides. We were empowered by learning Reiki or other energy healing techniques.

But now the transition is done. Living Post-New-Age, we can definitely avoid breaking today's vibrational rules. Again, I'll be showing you how.

3. Psychological overwork

PSYCHOLOGICAL OVERWORK results from going overboard on self-growth... until psychological probing becomes a habit. A common motivation goes, "Once I get to the bottom of my issues, life will be great."

Such an appealing hope! Back in the Age of Faith, so many smart people found this appealing. Yet what were the results? More often than not, people were working so hard on themselves, they couldn't see how (outside their own heads) they were acting more stuck than ever.

With today's new vibrational freedom, the consequences are even worse: psychological overwork. You will learn more about this consciousness lifestyle in Part Three. Where, as always, our emphasis will be on finding practical solutions.

4. Human-based spirituality

For a happy middle-ground, choose HUMAN-BASED SPIRITUALITY. With this consciousness lifestyle, emphasis is placed on your human life. No more reading energies all day long or begging spirits for guidance or perpetually working on your issues. Neither is personal growth resisted in the manner of spiritual shutdown.

Instead you move forward faster on your path of personal development. How fast? As fast as is *humanly* possible. And that involves making...

Two Kinds of Choice

Everyday life on earth has never been as complicated as it is now. We are faced with a wide array of HORIZONTAL CHOICES. These involve human frequencies, choices right at the surface of life. For instance, which kind of workout will make you happier, basketball or kickboxing?

Besides that, knowingly or not, in this Age of Awakening we can now make VERTICAL CHOICES. While putting on your left shoe, will your awareness stay on the physical reality of that shoe? Or will you float into astral-type experiences (a.k.a., "Daydreaming"), inwardly multi-tasking while you put on that shoe?

No longer does awareness automatically stay put at human frequencies. Living now, at any time, we can delve deeper into experience, like opening up the big Matroyshka doll and pulling out a smaller, cuter equivalent.

But what happens when we play around too much at astral vibrational frequencies? We stop taking personal responsibility. Ignoring our human lives, one day at a time, also adds up to a pattern, a not-so-great consciousness lifestyle. In the Age of Awakening, it's no longer automatic that you will live in human-based spirituality. (Although you sure can!)

How to Improve Your Consciousness Lifestyle

Here's the secret for moving into human-based spirituality: **20 DAILY MINUTES OF TECHNIQUE TIME, TOPS.**

What is TECHNIQUE TIME? It's your time for personal development. Dedicated time.

When not doing that official Technique Time, you simply live your life. Trust me, you'll find plenty of other things to interest you, human-type things.

The Technique Time solution can help you to overcome both psychological overwork and spiritual addiction. It's even a way to move past spiritual shutdown. For today's human-based spirituality, daily Technique Time is essential. Sounds interesting, doesn't it? You can start this consciousness lifestyle today. How?

1. Schedule into each day a 20-minute period for experimenting with energy, analyzing your life, seeking God, whatever.

2. Before starting that day's Technique Time, decide how you will use it. Maybe 5 minutes of prayer, 10 minutes of analyzing a recent conversation that triggered your emotions, 5 minutes of energy healing. You decide.

3. Do whichever combo you like... for as long as 20 minutes, by the clock. No more.

4. Then that day's Technique Time is *over*. Accept that. "Today's supply is used up." Do no more than 20 minutes per day, and no cheating.

5. What will you do for the rest of your waking hours? Live your regular human life: Say things. Do things. Accomplish things. Learn things (human-type things).

Sure you can live this way. Experiment for three weeks and then evaluate the results. I think you'll be impressed. If so, you can decide to continue that experiment long term. I sure have. For more specifics, skip ahead to Part Five.

Incidentally, right at the start of this book, did you notice a few pages with success stories? These came from people who used to live in spiritual addiction, psychological overwork, or spiritual shutdown. Now they live in human-based spirituality.

They did it, and you can too. If you revisit those quotes now, you may be inspired. What else may inspire you?

Our Age of Awakening Isn't New Age.
We're Living Post-New-Age.

A thousand years ago — even a hundred years back — there was just one consciousness lifestyle, human-based spirituality. (At least unless there was mental illness or a person took drugs.) Why did that come so automatically? People lacked the vibrational freedom that all of us have today.

So which consciousness lifestyles were very rare? Spiritual shutdown, spiritual addiction, and psychological overwork. Sure they were possible, but these problems developed only after concerted effort for very long periods of time, many years. Remember, from a vibrational perspective, it didn't used to matter much where we directed attention; the veil remained thick, keeping awareness nearly always stuck at human frequencies.

For example, a person could choose to "Think positive" versus "Grouse and grump." But this was human-type thinking, mentally substituting nicer emotions and ideas for spontaneous reactions.

Ever hear of the mega-bestseller "The Power of Positive Thinking"? Published in 1952 by Dr. Norman Vincent Peale, this self-help book contained references to God. Yet vibrationally it appealed to human-level awareness. Included were comforting thoughts of divinity, not a method for having direct experience of the Divine. Here's a typical quote:

"Stand up to an obstacle. Just stand up to it, that's all, and don't give way under it, and it will finally break. You will break it. Something has to break, and it won't be you, it will be the obstacle."

Human based, right?

By 1952, the veil had been thinning significantly. Then, during the **NEW AGE YEARS**, from 1980 to December 21, 2012, that veil began thinning faster than ever. Finally, like a tiny cosmic click, the Shift happened. All humans began living in the Age of Awakening.

During those transitional years, much in New Age spirituality went mainstream and helped people like you and me to start dealing with our greater energy sensitivity. For example, a different version of "Think positive" was introduced, via an astral source channeled by Esther Hicks. Her Law of Attraction bestsellers encouraged people to "dreamboard" etc. at astral vibrational frequencies, often giving rise to spiritual addiction.

During these New Age years, the two other troubling consciousness lifestyles began to appear occasionally (noticed in my work with clients, for instance). People developed psychological overwork or spiritual shutdown, and why? Seems to me, they needed to experiment in all sorts of ways because they felt so very uncomfortable adjusting to their increasingly intense, new, energy sensitivity.

What about now, when we're finally living in the Age of Awakening? Many transitional approaches to self-growth do not work as well as before; they can even slow down personal growth. And with the veil gone completely, problems with consciousness lifestyle can develop very rapidly.

Because times have changed, you might wish to evaluate what you do for Technique Time. Some forms of personal development may have been more appropriate during the New Age years. With all due gratitude, you may choose to move on and find different techniques to help you.

Making this kind of assessment is intensely personal. Maybe a relief. Maybe hard. Maybe both. Yet you may find this discernment indispensable for shaping your chosen consciousness lifestyle.

In case it helps, here's an analogy. If you were pregnant you might do a lot of things for personal growth. While you carrying your child, perhaps you'd get a copy of "What to Expect While You're Expecting." Then you'd diligently follow all recommendations.

But after giving birth, wouldn't you'd start to use different recommendations, develop new skills?

Collectively, humanity has given birth. No longer are we preparing for a new age. We're living it.

I'm here to help you develop a knack for comfortable living that helps you succeed in this Age of Awakening. Limiting Technique Time is needed because you live now, not in a past which was governed by yesterday's vibrational rules.

Leadership Opportunities

Powerfully Human Reader, by now you've probably realized why The New Strong is so new. It involves adjusting to a vibrational freedom that simply wasn't available in past decades. Or centuries. Or even millennia.

While vibrational balance takes more than choosing a consciousness lifestyle, that part isn't optional. Maybe you're worrying, though. Could 20 daily minutes really be enough for you to grow fast? Because you're not a hobbyist, not some dilettante. You really, really care.

Well, the answer is yes. Those 20 minutes will do the job nicely. Actually you may be amazed how much faster you grow, how much stronger you feel. Don't take my word for it. Experiment for a few weeks, then assess the results. Give yourself the benefit of this simple experiment. And I'll mention right now, you might also do it for the sake of helping others.

Have you ever heard of **THE HUNDREDTH MONKEY EFFECT?** Leadership from early adopters can uplift others who aren't quite so awake. Another way to put this comes from the great psychiatrist Carl Jung. He wrote about **COLLECTIVE CONSCIOUSNESS,** how all human beings are connected in our spiritual evolution. Moving into The Age of Awakening signals a great leap for humanity's collective consciousness.

What's the greatest new possibility on earth now, with the veil gone? Enlightenment is becoming attainable for millions of us.

ENLIGHTENMENT means an everyday state of consciousness where you are living your full potential, strongly connected to spiritual source. Energetically, in a spontaneous way, you're of greatest possible service to others. Living The New Strong can help get you there.

Powerfully Human Reader, whether or not you're interested in Enlightenment, you're living in a new era when you have no choice about whether your consciousness lifestyle matters. Living today, consequences are inescapable — like having a lifestyle around technology.

A thousand years ago, or even 150 years ago, who needed a technology lifestyle? Well, times have changed a bit, haven't they?

Today who doesn't accept that they must deal with technology? Yet relatively few people know there is such a thing as a consciousness lifestyle, or that you can purposely make choices about it. The knowledge you have just received can help you to become a leader.

Living in human-based spirituality, you can inspire others and even contribute to collective consciousness. Of course you might just be interested in strengthening *yourself* vibrationally. Either way, it's important to not just slip-slide into a random consciousness lifestyle. Because you, and you alone, will face the consequences of your choice.

What, can it weaken you to unintentionally slip into an imbalanced consciousness lifestyle? Think I'm kidding? In our next chapter, I'll give you an example to wrap up Part Two of this Program for Easy Vibrational Balance.

CHAPTER 10

A Pretty Expensive Sunhat

Powerfully Human Reader, we're about to conclude our first practical coaching in how to play by the rules of the Age of Awakening. In our last few chapters you learned about a trio of risks to your consciousness lifestyle:

- ∾ Too much playing with energy as today's shiny new toy.
- ∾ The Romance of the Astral.
- ∾ Consciousness lifestyles that limit personal growth.

Another highlight of Part Two was your introduction to 20 Daily Minutes of Technique Time, Tops — a simple way to strengthen yourself vibrationally.

Now let's put a human face on the ideas that have been discussed so far. Here's a teaching tale that presents...

A New Age "Miracle"

With reverence Ted recounted an event that changed his life. To him, it was a miracle. To me? Something else. I'll sum up his story so that you can decide for yourself.

One Sunday, Ted and his wife, Nellie, took a day trip to a nearby lake. In the gift shop, he bought her a lovely new sunhat in a gorgeous shade of blue. Although this gift store item was pricey, it looked great on her. He thought that bit of indulgence would make a perfect souvenir of their perfect day.

Then Ted and Nellie rented a rowboat and took it out on the lake. They were having so much fun, until a gust of wind blew that sunhat clean off Nellie's head. With a sinking sensation, they watched their extravagant little souvenir disappear into the water.

They tried, and failed, to fish that sunhat out of the lake. Although the rest of the day was still lovely, Nellie and Ted both felt disappointed.

So imagine Ted's surprise the next day! After coming home from work, he opened the trunk of his car to take out a package. There in plain sight was Nellie's sunhat. It looked fresh and new. And dry. Unmistakably it was the exact same souvenir, in that gorgeous shade of blue.

What a miracle! How could this have happened?

When Ted closed his eyes to reflect, an angel introduced himself. His name was Sam. He was the one who had retrieved the hat. This was done to demonstrate how eager he was to help Ted. To help Ted in every way, great and small.

From now on, all Ted had to do was close his eyes, go inside, and ask for advice. As his guardian angel, Sam would give Ted sacred guidance. And if Ted accepted that help, his life would become so much better.

Ted was thrilled. When he gave the sunhat back to Nellie, she was puzzled at first, then delighted.

For Ted, what happened was a much bigger deal than the mere return of a hat. Sam's miracle became a turning point in Ted's life. All day long, Ted asks Sam what to do and then follows all advice religiously.

Ted believes that his life is graced now. Never hurried, he stops to notice the beautiful energies all around him. Why worry about a thing?

A bubble of security surrounds him, and Ted has faith that everything will always work out for the best. "Because I am always in touch with my Spiritual Source."

Well, that's one interpretation. And it's clear that Ted does feel very graced. I've met him. He displays an impressive serenity.

But What's Happening Vibrationally?

Is Ted's new lifestyle really just another spiritual success story?

Pulling a sunhat out of a lake. Drying it off. Delivering it in a car trunk. Doing all that definitely qualifies as special, in an Other-Sidey kind of way. But does that necessarily add up to a miracle orchestrated by God Almighty?

No, not in my opinion. This was the work of an astral being. Doing a job like this is easier for spirits now, either singly or with a group. Even while the veil was thick, ghosts in creaky old castles have been able to move around objects. With today's vibrational flow, producing a trick like this has become far easier.

Sure, that sunhat caper took effort. But didn't Sam's investment pay off nicely? Ted is now taking orders from him all day long. One human soul's loyalty, purchased for the price of a sunhat!

Powerfully Human Reader, can you see why the new rules matter so much? Post-New-Age, playing around with energies can become so enticing that people can easily lose perspective. Sure, Ted can commune with angels all day long, but does that make it smart? Ted's aura shows that he lives in spiritual addiction, and this will continue until he chooses to live differently.

My advice to you? Choose a consciousness lifestyle that brings you great support of nature, not a pleasant astral haze.

You Can Begin Your Chosen Lifestyle Today

Human-based spirituality gives you the best of all the other three lifestyles, but in a balanced way.

~ *Security.* (A very human desire that doesn't have to produce spiritual shutdown.)

⇛ *Questing* for something spiritual, even for the Divine. (A kind of nobility that need not result in spiritual addiction.)

⇛ *Striving* for self-understanding. (An aspiration that propels so many honest seekers of truth into psychological overwork, but could be used far more productively.)

The alternative can be simple. *Stay interested in your human life.* When problems arise, solve them in human ways rather than trying to game the system. And keep your Technique Time to 20 minutes per day, maximum.

The New Strong is lived by accepting today's new vibrational rules. Automatically you'll start feeling more secure. (Probably less anxious, as well.) And if you're ambitious about personal growth, you'll be able to tell the difference.

If you favor the astral, you can enjoy astral flash, just like Ted. Just be prepared for an ever-growing gap between your inner buzz versus getting respect from others who aren't also in spiritual addiction.

By contrast, what will happen if you choose to value your human life, first and foremost? You will gain good, clean support from the astral. And also the Divine.

Maybe you're wondering, could human-based spirituality bring you psychological benefits as well?

PART THREE

Today's Well-Adjusted Human, PSYCHOLOGICALLY

Sigmund Freud would be so impressed with us. Never could he have imagined how regular people like us, in this age, would be able to access our subconscious minds. Or how Post-New-Age perceptiveness might help us change our lives for the better.

Back then, the great psychoanalyst still managed to change human life in a way that was pretty amazing. Little more than a century ago, Dr. Freud was just getting started. In 1901 he published "The Psychopathology of Everyday Life," which first popularized knowledge of the subconscious mind and related discoveries that have since gone mainstream.

For example, the FREUDIAN SLIP was one of his mind-boggling discoveries. When *hadn't* people made little speech errors? But Freud gets credit for investigating how certain slips of the tongue are not random but, instead, hint at deeper feelings and beliefs. Through Freudian slips, subconscious material can present itself in the midst of everyday life.

This discovery, alone, was such a breakthrough. Yet it was only one of Freud's genius discoveries. All of them resulted from coura-geously delving into his patients' subconscious experiences, a.k.a. "Unconscious" experiences.

Back then, psychiatrists didn't know that the vibrational nature of life on the planet was changing. Yet the veil was thinning com-pared to centuries past. This is why it became possible to think in the terms that shaped modern psychological thought.

Even so, it's to Freud's credit that he helped patients to purposely explore their subconscious minds; then Freud developed theories to make sense of those findings. Writing and teaching, he changed collective consciousness forever.

In his fascination with the mind's potential, Freud used hypnotism. For a couple of years he also experimented with cocaine, which he considered a way to boost his "self-control." From a vibrational perspective, what happened was a bit different. Cocaine gave Freud access to frequencies beyond human-level experience — astral frequencies — and temporarily put *that* in control. (Also, sadly, depositing plenty of STUFF in his aura, as such recreational drugs always do.)

Living today, we can only imagine how heroically Freud and his patients struggled, seeking buried treasures of psychological insight. By contrast, fast forward to today. Slip-sliding into subconscious experience isn't the least bit rare. Anyone with average intelligence can do it. And does. Innumerable times every day.

For instance, the last time you shopped at a supermarket, where was consciousness positioned for your fellow shoppers? Most likely, many were involved in their habitual pursuit of self-growth … which contributed to their psychological overwork. (Without knowing what was going on, you may have been doing a bit of that kind of thing yourself.)

Yes, Freud came to fame with a book called "The Psychopathology of *Everyday Life*." Today we could fill many books with "The Psychopathology Caused by *Too Much Psychological Focus in Everyday Life*."

In Part Three you will make new discoveries about how, in this Age of Awakening, you can become better adjusted psychologically. Better adjusted because of how you position your Post-New-Age consciousness.

CHAPTER 11

Psychology in the Age of Awakening

So far, Powerfully Human Reader, we've explored today's new vibrational rules in terms of spirituality. You have begun to understand the importance of a healthy consciousness lifestyle. Now let's talk psychology, because today's new vibrational rules definitely impact psychological growth.

Bottom line? Practices that used to strengthen you psychologically might weaken you now, while a slight shift in emphasis can help you to gain The New Strong.

- Do you speak the language of psychology even more than you speak the language of spirituality? Here come practical insights.
- And what if you are used to speaking both languages, *psychology* and *spirituality*? Soon I'll help you put them together in a way that may be very new to you, and very meaningful.

What does it mean psychologically that "The veil has thinned"? How do today's new rules impact the work that you're doing on yourself?

Discoveries about vibrational frequencies have huge implications for **SELF-ACTUALIZATION**, which is humanistic psychologist Abraham Maslow's concept of living from your true self. You can aim for that in a manner that mobilizes today's new rules. So let's examine why your consciousness lifestyle could become so relevant to your psychological self-actualization.

Psychologically What HASN'T Changed

Powerfully Human Reader, do you remember the first time you learned the remarkable idea that you have a "Subconscious mind"?

Maybe your **CONSCIOUS MIND** doesn't remember. That's perfectly normal. Conscious thinking could be defined as "What you notice here and now, plus what you can remember off the top of your head."

Plenty of daily experiences aren't recalled, but so what? This limitation is, actually, desirable. It helps keep you sane. Effective human life requires that you consciously use only a small fraction of total mental capacity.

Why? No matter how motivated you may be to access every possible memory, what would happen if your mind *didn't* default to conscious vibrational frequencies?

For instance, what would it be like to cross a city street if you were busy remembering all the memories from this day alone? Amid all that overwhelming data, you might not bother to notice puny little details like oncoming cars.

So you depend on that life-saving conscious mind. Still there's more to you mentally: a subconscious mind that is way bigger and more comprehensive.

Somewhere deep in your memory lies a recollection of the first time that you heard that term "**SUBCONSCIOUS MIND**." Of course, that long-ago memory lives within you. Because *everything* that has happened to you lives there, stored as a memory.

Subconscious information is hidden from the conscious mind. By design, you don't have to pay attention to those innumerable details.

What does it take for you to clearly access subconscious knowledge? You must slip into an altered state of awareness, quite different from everyday conscious thinking.

Ten thousand years ago, Indian researchers of awareness described the *chit*, or STOREHOUSE OF IMPRESSIONS, within the subconscious mind.

This contains detailed memories of everything you have ever seen, heard, touched, smelled, or tasted; also whatever has been overheard, seen with peripheral vision; felt, liked, disliked, not cared about one way or another, or purposely ignored. All of that lies within you right now.

Those ancient experts on human consciousness also believed in REINCARNATION, which means having a succession of lifetimes as part of each soul's evolution.

Accordingly, your storehouse of impressions contains a complete history of everything you have experienced as a soul, every incident from every lifetime, plus every incident between lifetimes (when you have been living in a heaven, inhabiting an astral world appropriate to your level of consciousness).

Powerfully Human Reader, when there's so much you can't consciously remember, it can be reassuring to know that doesn't make your memory bad. If you aim to find some of that buried information, that's definitely possible.

Suppose that you'd like to remember where you put a valuable watch right before losing it. You can engage the services of a professional hypnotist who specializes in knowledge retrieval.

All professional hypnotists are experts at using the power of the subconscious mind to help people solve everyday problems. Forensic hypnotists specialize in helping people to remember important details from the past, even testimony accurate enough to be admissible in court.

Don't you find it comforting that your subconscious mind never forgets? I love this idea. It's like owning the most immense storage locker imaginable, way bigger than the Internet or cloud computing. Plus this storage locker has been given to you for free.

To round out your collection of attentional resources, the third level within you is the **HIGHER SELF**. This is the wise mind within. It looks out for the rest of you.

Wonderful though your Higher Self and subconscious mind are, living today there's a catch.

Something tricky! Something that involves your sense of loyalty....

Being Yourself Authentically

Used to be, the conscious mind stayed in charge automatically. People didn't worry, "Who is the real me?" Regarding personal identity, you had about as much choice as buyers of the Model T Ford: "Any customer can have a car painted any colour that he wants so long as it is black."

In the days of Henry Ford, America's most famous car manufacturer, your best choice *in life* was to act like a stand-up human being. Otherwise, you could flout tradition and defy authority, refusing to do your duty. Trouble would follow.

That simple.

Simple vibrationally, anyhow. You had few vertical choices, right?

In this Age of Awakening, far more complicated! You can readily experience any of the three levels of human consciousness. Therefore, you have colorful choices about what it means to "Be yourself" or "Feel authentic."

- Because of how awareness flows now, you might prefer to put your Higher Self in charge.
- Or aim to make your subconscious conscious.

Many people deliberately strive in these ways. How about you? Does your search for authenticity aim to improve upon ordinary human-level, conscious awareness?

If so, you're invited to reconsider.

Your *conscious mind* connects you to objective reality, helping you to act and react appropriately.

That conscious mind directs your free will, helping you to connect with people as you wish, to do your best at time management, to enjoy your life as much as possible.

Does that impress you? Or do you feel more like, "Been there, done that. Now I want something more sophisticated to be in charge?"

Meanwhile your *subconscious mind* stores every single memory, no matter how small, just in case you might need it. Plus, your subconscious takes care of running your mind-body-system.

- An excellent example is your autonomic nervous system, which regulates functions like breathing and heartbeat.
- Another example: Involuntary muscles create authentic facial expressions without your having to manage them consciously in order to "look authentic."

Actually there's a long list of jobs for which your subconscious mind is responsible, not your conscious mind. With all that mysterious complexity, does your subconscious mind seem like the most valuable part? Would you prefer to put this in charge, rather than your conscious mind?

For instance, maybe Freudian slips are evidence of your subconscious mind trying to break through in a way that would help you. Could your subconscious reactions be more authentic, wilder and more free than humdrum conscious thinking?

I'd take that with a grain of salt. Human-reality-type salt. Your subconscious mind already has plenty to do. Really you know better than to wish that the collaboration between conscious and subconscious thinking would change from how it already works.

Now, what about the job of your *Higher Self*? Whenever life-changing guidance is needed, your Higher Self whispers the wisdom. This is gently done, except for emergencies. This magnificent part of you doesn't need to resort to pushy, in-your-face, daily guidance.

Nor does your Higher Self boss your conscious mind around in any way. The goal is not to detract from your conscious free will but to enhance it. Still, would it be preferable to live from your Higher Self, put that in charge all day long? Does "Higher" mean "more authentic"?

Powerfully Human Reader, why would a sensible person want to do that? Send your Higher Self to the drugstore, perhaps, to select the ultimate cosmic toothpaste from the various products displayed?

There is no cosmic toothpaste to buy. Yet I've stopped counting how many first-time clients, idealists all, have told me, "I want to live from my Higher Self." Powerfully Human Reader, even *attempting* to do this will mess a person up pretty good. As a human being, you'll do better if you live and let live:

- Accept that your conscious mind does the work of your conscious mind.
- Allow your subconscious mind to do just the work of your subconscious mind.
- Be grateful that your Higher Self does only the work of your Higher Self.

Today's rules support that correct choice, that loyalty. Still, where do your loyalties lie? For instance, seeking to live from your Higher Self might seem like the ultimate expression of appreciation and gratitude.

As for the allure of subconscious insight, does it seem too tempting to resist? Might you feel like you can't help yourself? Do you probe your subconscious mind at every opportunity, seeking a kind of psychological truth that will set you free?

If so, I recommend that you turn to our next chapter immediately.

CHAPTER 12

When "Psychological" Equals "Vibrational"

Living now, you can favor your subconscious mind or your Higher Self... not your conscious mind... to a degree that simply was not possible before the Age of Awakening.

Where will your loyalties lie? Only you can decide.

To inform you further, let's add a startling correlation. Each of these three levels within you, named *psychologically*, corresponds to a vibrational frequency that can also be named *metaphysically*.

That's right, in this particular context, the language of spirituality (or metaphysics) translates exactly into the language of psychology. Here's the deal:

- Your conscious mind (psychologically) = Human frequencies (spiritually)
- Your subconscious mind (psychologically) = Astral frequencies (spiritually)
- Your Higher Self (psychologically) = Divine frequencies (spiritually)

How can that correlation help you to evaluate ideals like authenticity, loyalty, sense of self? Let's flesh out these three vital equivalencies.

Subjective Reality and Objective Reality at the CONSCIOUS Level

Quick question, Powerfully Human Reader. How would you define **OBJECTIVE REALITY**?

When I ask clients, sometimes they give answers like these:

- Adam: Objective reality is everything I notice happening.
- Natalie: Objective reality is whatever seems important to me.
- Holden: Objective reality? That doesn't really exist. Everybody has a different version.

Clever answers all! Unfortunately definitions like these mean trouble. Because it matters enormously how you define ordinary, everyday physical reality. Answers like these might work brilliantly in a graduate seminar for philosophers, but they won't help you earn a living in most kinds of work. And definitely don't try to work as a lawyer.

How about this? For practical purposes, objective reality means physical objects, things that can be measured and counted, what people and animals say and do, plus what would show on a YouTube video.

And guess what? This kind of objective reality is available exclusively at conscious-level, human-type, vibrational frequencies. It does not exist at astral or Divine vibrational levels, where "things" are made out of energy.

Besides objective reality, your conscious mind can also experience SURFACE SUBJECTIVE REALITY:

- How you *feel* about life's surface objective reality.
- What you *think* about objective reality.
- How you feel and think about *your* subjective experiences.
- What *other people* feel and think, far as you can tell from surface-level reality; like how you interpret their facial expressions and body language.
- How *you* feel and think about other people's surface subjective reality.

~ Attempting to help people by acting in a supportive manner through *speech and action.*

Plenty to keep you humanly busy, right? Even without slip-sliding into the astral.

At Your SUBCONSCIOUS Level, a Different Reality

For practical purposes, there is no "Objective Reality" at the subconscious level. You will not find well-polished tables, horses with flesh-and-blood nostrils aquiver, or a traffic light that turns red (which could precede your being ticketed by a police officer).

Instead, **DEEP SUBJECTIVE EXPERIENCE** is experienced at the subconscious level. Meaning what?

~ How you feel, think, react, and interpret when *not fully engaged with objective reality* in present time.

~ Memories, dreams, reflections, free associations, where *anything that you notice can feel true.*

~ *Processing* emotions, savoring them, or wishing that you didn't have them.

~ How you notice other people's *energies.* (And your own.)

~ Whenever you aim to *understand more deeply* what makes other people tick.

Reality at Your HIGHER SELF Level

At the **HIGHER SELF** level, experience is also subjective only. Yet this kind of experience differs from qualities of experience at the subconscious level.

Higher Self means **THE WONDERFUL COUNSELOR** within, the greatest wisdom that can guide you.

Psychologists have developed many names for this, including **THE IDEAL SELF** (Carl Rogers) and **THE WISE MIND** (Marsha Linehan).

What might you experience through your Higher Self?

- ᷁ Making contact with your *highest inner wisdom.*
- ᷁ Subjective knowledge of *truth principles,* and how they apply to everyday situations.
- ᷁ *Hunches* to do something (or to not do something).
- ᷁ *Co-creation* with the greatest inner source of love, light, and power.
- ᷁ Spiritual *transcendence.*
- ᷁ Resolving problems in a way that brings *a lasting peace.*
- ᷁ *Self-actualization,* as described by Abraham Maslow.
- ᷁ Or *Enlightenment,* as described by wisdom traditions from the East.

That Higher Self sounds great, doesn't it? Living The New Strong brings you the clearest possible access to your Higher Self, and also to your subconscious mind… when you go there during Technique Time.

As for the rest of your waking hours, your amazing conscious mind is in charge. Juicy!

You see, like any good thing in life, the deeper forms of consciousness can be pursued in ways that bring you support of nature. Or not.

Most of us would like to be wise and also wealthy. Although there are legitimate ways to seek wealth, there are also ways that might cause a person to live in jail for a while. Prison isn't likely, due to breaking today's rules about positioning consciousness. But what is?

CHAPTER 13

Tempted by Psychological Overwork?

Ever since the veil dissolved, it has become child's play for someone like you or me to access subconscious material. No psychiatrist's couch needed!

Fascinating though it is when awareness slip-slides into subconscious vibrational frequencies, ask yourself: *Just because it feels good, does that make it smart?*

Psychological overwork is the unintended consequence of too much time spent analyzing life, rather than living it. With all due respect, your personal growth does not depend on how perceptive you are. What does matter for personal growth? Where you routinely position your consciousness.

Here's another way to think of it: Restraint. In this Age of Awakening, restraint and finesse can help you as never before. A very little self-analysis goes a long way. While spending more than 20 minutes each day analyzing your life *will* — not *may* — produce psychological overwork.

How does this show in a person's aura? Energetic literacy reveals imbalance similar to the distressing results of spiritual addiction.

Before the Age of Awakening, people could get away with far more self-scrutiny; even then, though, too much do-it-yourself self-shrinking caused problems. Think of all those jokes you've heard about the messed-up children of therapists.

Personally you may have known some diehard analyzers who would punctuate much of your conversation by asking, "How does that make you feel?" As if naming feelings would cure all of life's ills!

Still, those annoyances were mild, and rare, compared with what's happening now for millions of people: Drifting farther and farther away from reality, despite thinking they're helping themselves.

Yet this vicious cycle can quickly start spinning in the other direction, towards an excellent adjustment to life in the Age of Awakening. The lifestyle of psychological overwork can certainly be changed into habits that support human-based spirituality.

Gain Support of Nature Like a Really Smart Person

The very smartest people know better than trying to fight the laws of nature. Rather than endless analyzing, you can enjoy applying your ingenuity towards enjoying your life and, maybe, helping others.

Please don't think in terms of *overcoming* the psychological over-work. For instance, don't use your precious Technique Time to analyze what caused your current consciousness lifestyle. Instead, change it. Just follow these five simple steps.

1. Adapt to the time in history when you are living. What works now for self-growth? During most of your waking hours, spontaneously say things and do things, whether alone or with others. That simple! (Automatically this will position your consciousness for the fastest personal growth.)

2. Human experience may not seem perfect but let it be good enough. What if you prefer the mysteries of your subconscious mind and Higher Self? Consider that a habit you can retire. It's out of date. By contrast, in the Age of Awakening, psychological health is lived in the now.

3. What if you're still curious about the depths of your being? Good! Explore that during your 20 Daily Minutes of Technique Time (Tops).

4. Commit to living in reality, not self-analysis. You know the difference.

5. Putting human life first will soon feel natural. Don't worry if that change of emphasis feels a bit awkward while you're still getting used to it.

"But, but, but." If you feel resistance to any of this, it's understandable. You invested a lot in working on yourself. Well, maybe it's time to reap the rewards.

You may be pleasantly surprised at what happens, once you muster the sense of adventure to muddle through each day as a human-style being, warts and all. Then your conscious mind will learn from consequences in objective reality; and all the while, your subconscious mind and Higher Self will integrate this personal growth.

Living now, you can progress so rapidly towards psychological self-actualization. Just do your reasonable best as a human being and see what happens. This next teaching tale may inspire you.

A Single Mother's Triumph

My client Bridget thoroughly understands the importance of choosing a consciousness lifestyle. For years she suffered from a significant spiritual addiction. Overcoming that helped her to make enormous progress towards actualizing herself as a person.

Yet being a single mother remained really hard. Since she had to deal with so many problems, Bridget often felt overwhelmed.

What happened next? Knowing better than to return to spiritual addiction, Bridget inadvertently slipped into psychological addiction. For instance, off and on she would contemplate topics like, "What is motivating that awful childcare provider?"

Repeatedly Bridget was reminded to stick to 20 Daily Minutes of Technique Time, Tops. Eventually, human-based spirituality became comfortable. Since then, her personal progress has accelerated rapidly.

But not everyone receives clear coaching from one-on-one sessions with an RES practitioner. On their own, people can find psychological overwork hard to recognize. The following examples can help you get the idea.

These Hardworking Self-Actualizers Had No Clue

Slip-sliding into psychological overwork is so darned common these days. Do you know anyone like these hard-working folks?

- Jasper changed after his divorce, resolving to take full responsibility for all his problems. Serious responsibility. No more blaming his ex! Relentlessly responsible, Jasper accepts no excuses. Soon as a negative thought comes up, he sticks with it, feeling it deeply. Jasper won't stop until he identifies what he feels, no matter how scary. Exhausting? Yes, but Jasper's ideals keep him going. "Eventually all my work will pay off, and there will be an end to this mess." (He thinks.)

- Jane has been into self-analysis ever since childhood. Although she has never seen a therapist, Jane knows she would make a great one, and proves it by monitoring her emotions constantly. At work, even while talking to customers, Jane is secretly doing her "real" work: trying to stay emotionally balanced; searching for causes of distress; exploring traumas buried deep in her past. "This is helping me grow super-fast." (She thinks.)

- Joe worries about his anger. Many times each day, resentment rips through him. Immediately Joe struggles to work through those negative emotions, asking himself, "Why do I feel this way?" When alone, he drops everything else to continue his brave self-analysis. Even with others, Joe often withdraws into his private world of pain, secretly working on himself. "Once all this work is done, I'll feel better." (He thinks.)

~~ James strives to live from his Higher Self. Everyday reality has shifted into a thrilling quest for ultimate truth. Often James asks himself, What is the real meaning here?" And although he wouldn't say it out loud, it's clear to him, "Ordinary life can never satisfy somebody as psychologically advanced as me." (He thinks.)

Just How Productive Is All that Psychological Work?

Bless their hearts. Jasper, Jane, Joe, and James all work so hard. Each of their specialties for self-growth became possible because the veil vanished. (Even if nobody sent them the memo.)

Years ago, their self-inquiry would have been harder. Less interesting, too. Now it's totally effortless for them to slip-slide into subconscious material, in all its infinite variety. The sense of discovery has intensified.

How seductive this is — especially when combined with belief that all the inner work will pay off. No wonder, folks like James are going off the deep end without knowing it. What is accomplished through all that earnest psychological striving? Does it really make these people better, more whole? Sadly, no.

And from a Vibrational Perspective

Here is what I have learned, over and over, from helping RES clients. Delving into subconscious material without help from a skilled mental health expert — this does not usually help people to progress much — beyond pursuing a meaningful hobby.

For example, Joe is correct about having a lot of anger. And he's so wise to do something about it. But will he really fix that problem on his own by "Working through his feelings"?

Not professionally trained as a psychotherapist, Joe doesn't know this basic fact: even professional therapists don't work on themselves. When they need help, therapists go to *other* mental health professionals.

Why do they spend the money? Because they know it's a smart investment. Mental health experts with different treatment models can offer really effective assistance.

From the contrasting perspective of RES, the true causes of Joe's anger are various kinds of subconscious-level STUFF, stored energetic garbage. Until this is gone for good, anger will keep erupting. Psychologically exploring those angry outbursts will not remove this STUFF, either. However, professional help to permanently heal STUFF can make a huge difference.

Of course RES practitioners aren't the only resources for energy healing. Other mind-body-spirit professionals can help too, bringing their various specialties. Smart consumers invest a smallish bit of time and money to accelerate their self-growth; again, a smart investment.

Yet sometimes a person prefers a do-it-yourself approach, and it's all that's needed. All four of the people described here could get some benefit from self-healing with this Program for Easy Vibrational Balance. Especially the part coming next!

CHAPTER 14

A Timely Solution

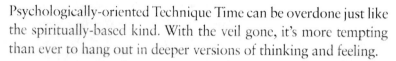

Psychologically-oriented Technique Time can be overdone just like the spiritually-based kind. With the veil gone, it's more tempting than ever to hang out in deeper versions of thinking and feeling.

These astral-level experiences can feel so good, causing a person to temporarily feel calmer, more spiritual, more balanced, less anxious. Which is great but so tempting to overdo.

Without warning, a person's sense of self begins to drift away from conscious human reality, moving towards an identity that isn't really about human life. Soon that person develops the habit of engaging in life with a subconscious or astral positioning of consciousness — playing with an interior Matroyshka doll, as it were.

Based on extensive research, I can summarize what energetic literacy reveals. What is the result of all that well-meant fixing, fixing, fixing? Either psychological overwork or spiritual addiction. Or both!

Fortunately I have found rapid normalization in the energy fields of people who spend just a few weeks reversing this vicious cycle. Here's a teaching tale to illustrate.

Benjamin, Loveable After All

Benjamin's best friend referred him to me as a client. Early in every session I research my client's aura to assess which type of STUFF is a priority to address for energy healing.

Long before I researched his aura, problems showed up. By our first two minutes together, I knew this session with Benjamin was going to be tough. Problems were so big that they showed right on the surface, not hidden within his energy field (as is the case with most of my clients).

Benjamin smirked. He sneered. And why did I notice Benjamin's mouth so much, anyway? Because his eyes appeared lifeless.

Researching his aura, the cause became clear. Benjamin was living a very extreme combination of psychological overwork and spiritual addiction. Would he accept my help?

It took all my professional composure to get through our session. Benjamin acted contemptuous, as if hardly listening to a thing I said. Somehow both of us persisted, though, and I managed to teach him the consciousness lifestyle skill that I'm going to help you to refine in this chapter, 20 Daily Minutes of Technique Time, Tops.

Benjamin expressed strong resistance to just about everything I said. After that session was over, I drew a deep breath and consoled myself with the thought that probably we would never speak again.

Surprisingly, a month later Benjamin returned for a follow-up appointment. Uh-oh!

Yet this time, soon as I saw Benjamin, my heart melted. This man was charming, very alive, with eyes that sparkled. Gone was all of that astral emphasis. Evidently a delightful person had been there all along, and now he was back.

Making This Consciousness Lifestyle Work for You

However involved you have become in your practices for personal growth, you too can benefit from keeping your Technique Time to 20 productive minutes each day.

There's an art to it, so we'll revisit this topic in Part Five of this book. Meanwhile you may be wondering, how can you possibly satisfy your desire to understand and analyze?

Here's one easy solution. Whenever you're in a situation that tempts you to analyze, do this. Send yourself a note via text message, summarizing the topic of interest. For instance:

- Why did I react that way on my date?
- What really motivated my boss when he talked to me like that?
- Me at the park. Feeling that old nostalgia. What was that about, exactly?

Right before your next session of Technique Time, look at those messages-to-self. Then act like an executive: set your priorities and enforce them. Yes, it can be that simple.

Instead of working on yourself all day long, you can use every Technique Time to develop brilliant, productive insights that really help you to grow. With today's vibrational freedom, that 20 minutes could be worth 5 days or more (if done 20 years ago).

What if questions arise during the rest of your waking hours? Aside from making quick notes, just deal. Muddle through that date. Manage that boss. Continue taking your walk at the park, no matter which emotions arise. (And maybe take time to smell the objective-reality roses.)

Playing up surface-level reality will strengthen you vibrationally. And what else? You may find yourself developing new human-type social skills, useful for solving problems.

People might like you better, too. Usually folks can tell when somebody like Joe is withdrawing. His "secret" ways of working on himself may not be so very secret after all.

What if you don't like texting notes to yourself? Find a substitute, like carrying around a small notebook where you jot down ideas.

Just don't keep your list mentally. That won't help, since you'll be tempted to review your list, off and on, all day long.

And you know what that inner review process would become, right? More Technique Time.

You see, Powerfully Human Reader, you really can keep it to 20 Daily Minutes of Technique Time, Tops. Doing that won't just help you avoid breaking today's new rules. You'll get better results from all your psychological self-help, spiritual seeking, the works.

Yet, for the very best results, there is more to learn. Certain kinds of astral-level STUFF can detract from your personal growth and, even, make it hard to stick to those 20 minutes daily. Wouldn't you like to do something about that?

Well, guess what's happening after we wrap up Part Three of this Program for Easy Vibrational Balance? Part Four will take a different approach for helping you to live The New Strong. Together we'll explore targeted skill sets for energetic self-healing.

PART FOUR

Vanquish
External Negative Energies

Here you are, Powerfully Human Reader, learning how to position consciousness in a way that brings you support of nature for living in this Age of Awakening.

Of course you can live this way. Just identify with *human* life, solve human problems *humanly*. As for seeking psychological insight or exploring awareness of energies, let that serve as the occasional supplement to your *human* life — never a substitute.

So here you are now, on a human-centered path that feels increasingly clean, balanced, and sane. You're learning to live The New Strong.

Now let's add to your understanding of how certain energies can have an impact. You see, in this Age of Awakening, the problem is not only how your awareness can move so fluidly between human and astral frequencies. More than ever before, negative energies from outside yourself can get stuck in your aura.

Energetic literacy research makes this crystal clear. Compared to before the Shift, more external negative energies are getting stuck in everyone's aura.

Certain energy-related forms of STUFF are very new. Subconsciously they are disruptive. Powerfully Human Reader, what can you do about that, rather than worry?

Let's be clear. There are not a gazillion kinds of external energies that impact most human beings today, just some very specific energy-related problems, every one of which is healable.

In Part Four, you're about to learn skill sets to vanquish those problems and protect yourself.

Once again, welcome to the Age of Awakening. Certain energy healing skills weren't much needed in the New Age years, but they sure can make a difference now.

CHAPTER 15

The Skill of Learning a Skill

STUFF is my name for it: stored emotional and energetic garbage in your aura or mine, at the astral level. As you know by now, this level within you corresponds to the subconscious mind.

In RES, our motto is: STUFF *can always, always, always be healed.*

Effective healing begins with discerning different kinds of STUFF. You see, particular things can get stuck in an aura, akin to golf balls versus meatballs versus wads of chewing gum. All this STUFF is definitely real. Except that astral objects are not real in a human-level way.

Things at an astral frequency exist as energies, and that's all. The only objects on earth with a solid, physical form exist at human vibrational frequencies.

So how do people without expert training learn about their STUFF? Mostly through experiencing the consequences of carrying that STUFF, such as human-type suffering.

Also, folks may sense that energetically something is amiss. Still, as I've mentioned before, random energy talk won't stop the suffering. For example, it won't help to blame a generalized culprit, like "bad energy" or "scary neon-green energy potatoes."

Removing different kinds of STUFF begins with being able to tell them apart. RES includes targeted skills, informed by full energetic literacy. Thanks to that, we now have knowledge of certain kinds of STUFF that are *new* in the Age of Awakening.

Targeted skill sets can remove these problems, just like different skills that I've developed and taught in earlier books in this series. Many old-'n-nasty kinds of STUFF can be removed with those other skills for self-healing.

In Part Four of this Program for Easy Vibrational Balance, you're going to learn several new self-healing skills sets. How will they work?

For each one, you'll receive step-by-step instructions. Always included will be a way to effortlessly position your consciousness to activate something within you called YOUR POWER OF COMMAND. This helps you to effectively clean up STUFF and then put into your aura what serves you better, helping you to express your soul more fully than ever.

No hard work will be needed to develop this Power of Command Because you are human, this capacity to heal yourself energetically is hardwired into you. When I help you to wake it up, your ordinary human speech will subtly morph into something far more spiritually potent.

Hold on. What if you never knew you had any Power of Command to activate? Nonetheless, that power still lies dormant within you, awaiting use. It allows you to co-create with the Divine.

It's an everyday kind of miracle, and always a sacred privilege, whenever human beings like us can effectively co-create healing based on teaming up with Divine vibrational frequency. (And then, of course, effective self-healing requires that we humans must add the rest of a specific skill set.)

How does Power of Command work, technically? Later you might wish to learn about that from Book One in the series about Energy HEALING Skills for the Age of Awakening, where you'll find a detailed explanation. For now, just benefit from *using* your Power of Command in this Book Four of that series.

Like all RES skill sets for energy healing, you will learn what to do step by step. To validate that a healing skill has worked, just see if you notice human-type results.

Powerfully Human Reader, before I start sharing these secrets for energetic self-healing, let's consider *how* best to learn. This chapter can add to your versatility with every one of the skills that you'll find in Part Four.

First Things First

All of us are busy these days. So that's taken into consideration for all the energy healing skills in this Program for Easy Vibrational Balance. Skill sets are designed to take just a minute or two, once you've learned them properly.

First I will teach you at depth. Learning the **TEACHING VERSION** of each new skill could take 20 minutes, as if we were sitting together in a workshop.

Afterwards you will be given a **QUICK VERSION**, where you'll just go through the motions of the skill set, surfacey and simple — no energy awareness needed.

Please don't skimp on that Teaching Version. It awakens your Power of Command, setting a pattern that integrates Divine and astral vibrational frequencies for the future. Skills are installed to help you from then on, every single time that you go through the steps of the skill set.

Actually, I think you'll enjoy when I lead you through the Teaching Version of a new skill. It can be fascinating. And it's good to know that one time through is all you need. After that depth learning, you will gain full results from using the Quick Version.

Now I won't be with you as you read, looking over your shoulder. Or, perhaps, smacking your hand with a ruler if you happen to misbehave. You alone will decide what to do; I can only advise you not to cheat yourself out of an immersion experience.

For instance, skimming with your eyes does not count as doing. If it helps, you could consider the Teaching Version of each skill set to be like a spiritual initiation.

And here's a bonus, vibrationally powerful. Occasionally (once a year, for example), you might revisit each Teaching Version. Then you can expect to go even deeper, with progressively clearer experiences. Doing this can give you the equivalent of an advanced workshop.

Good News about Technique Time

What's that good news? Although exploring the Teaching Version of a skill set will count as official Technique Time, doing the Quick Version will not. Having established a skill set, it's as though you have earned the standing to make that skill work quite automatically by humanly saying and doing the official sequence of steps.

When doing the Quick Version of a skill set, your awareness can stay positioned at regular human frequencies. Meanwhile your human job will just be to make certain physical movements and say certain words. (Really, you're doing more than that because of inner shifts that have been established by downloading the Teaching Version. Ha ha!)

Having gone through those motions, there will be no need to shift your vibrational positioning away from noticing regular, everyday human reality. How great is that! Frees up more of your Technique Time for that day, yet you get results from the skill set.

Collaborate Appropriately, Please

Instructions for many of the skill sets that follow will use the word "God."

Do you feel comfortable with that name? Rest assured that "God" will mean whichever version of the Divine *you* already know and trust, the God of your understanding.

Alternatively "God" can mean the version you wouldn't mind believing in… if you *did* believe in something like that. You see, an official belief is never required, merely a willingness to collaborate.

Now, what if you happen to dislike that word "God"? Just substitute one of the following alternatives:

- ⤳ Divine Goddess
- ⤳ Father-Mother God
- ⤳ The Love That Rules the Universe
- ⤳ The Intelligence That Rules the Universe
- ⤳ Highest Power. (That last name is an upgrade from "Higher Power," so popular in 12-Step Programs. "Highest Power" is far more suitable for our energy healing skill sets.)

Why do names like these matter so much? See Book One of the Energy HEALING Skills Series, especially Chapter 9.

Either Browse Or Do. Don't Spoil.

The first time you read through this book, it might seem tempting to skim through the Teaching Version of each skill set. Please don't. You're better off skipping that skill set entirely: go on to the next chapter.

Casual reading can spoil the effectiveness of instructions for learning these sacred skills. When you decide to actually learn, proceed slowly.

Do what is offered, no multi-tasking or shortcuts, adding no multiplication, subtraction, or long division.

Most people find there is one mind set, mood, or pacing for a *browse-through reading*, compared to *learning mode*. For many contexts in life, it won't matter which you do. Here it will.

That simple.

Stay Human, Please. Don't Get Trippy

From earlier chapters you know the importance of vibrational positioning at human frequencies. This is essential for our Program for Easy Vibrational Balance. (Likewise for every other skill set in RES.)

When energy healing is done, that doesn't mean you must get all infatuated with energy this or that. Space Cowboys, keep on your 10-gallon hat and everyday boots. (Or whatever human-type clothes you are wearing.) Resist any temptation to take a ride on energies as a substitute for human vibrational frequencies.

I'll help you position your consciousness appropriately. Simply follow instructions in the Teaching Version or Quick Version, and don't try to make things fancier than they need to be. Some of the skill sets you will learn are quite simple. Others will be more complex. Regardless, they're included because they really do work.

Depending on Your Background...

If you have prior training in RES skills

Book One in this series about Energy HEALING Skills explained how to use Five Cleaning Supplies to do a really superb job at STUFF removal. (That's "Use Your Power of Command for Spiritual Cleansing and Protection.")

This knowledge is specific to all the skills for self-healing in RES. With all respect, you will not have learned them in your training in other energy modalities, such as becoming a Reiki master or taking a clairvoyance workshop for psychic development or practicing Emotional Freedom Technique.

> If you have learned about these Five Cleaning Supplies, you'll recognize some of them in the Before-and-After Pictures that I'll be asking you to do. Know that you'll be using Your Power of Command whenever you speak the words of a healing.

⌇ You can also add two Vibe-Raising Breaths at the start and end of every technique in this book.

⌇ In a skill set with many parts you can add more Vibe-Raising Breaths before each new part.

⌇ Vibe-Raising Breaths are like salt. They make your experience tastier.

About skill multi-tasking

What if you have prior training in other modalities? Tempting though it may be to do **SKILL MULTI-TASKING**, resist. Layering one practice onto another is not a cute look, like wearing a sweater on top of your shirt.

Vibrationally the techniques in Part Four will clash with practices like these:

⌇ *Psychological modalities,* like acting as though you're with your therapist when you are not in a session but, rather you're on your own with this book. Working on your issues in any way counts as Technique Time. Not to be mixed in with the skills you learn here.

⌇ *Spiritual modalities,* like mindfulness meditation, trying to live from the heart, or attempting to stay positive. Also, while doing this Program for Easy Vibrational Balance, never try to watch yourself, or detach from an experience, or be "more spiritual" in any way.

⌇ *Energy modalities* for mind-body-spirit healing, like techniques of energy medicine such as Reiki, and energy psychology teachings like Emotional Freedom Technique.

⌇ Likewise avoid mixing in practices of *psychic development,* such as picking up messages or channeling or mediumship.

All this is really important. Otherwise you will not gain the expected results. To enjoy them, don't overcomplicate the straight-forward instructions provided.

If you don't have much background in energy anything

So much the easier for you, with no distracting habits: Powerfully Human Reader, do each skill set just as presented. Simple!

Perhaps you have background in purposely paying attention to yourself. Even if not, you've had a lifetime of spontaneously-noticed emotions and physical sensations. Casually paying attention — that's all I'm asking you to do in the before-and-after steps of a skill.

Pay attention to yourself in ordinary human ways. Nothing fancy, just a quick first thing you notice, nice and easy.

What, not probe for vibes, energies, experiences in your chakras, etc.? Nope. Please don't go there. Before-and-After Pictures in this program never mean paying attention to energy.

Did You Notice?

Powerfully Human Reader, instructions in this chapter exemplify good energy hygiene in this Age of Awakening.

Life improves enormously when you pay attention mostly to yourself *at human vibrational frequencies*. That means what happens in objective reality, plus your emotions and physical sensations that can be noticed without trying.

Yes, you can find plenty to notice that is human and NOT about energy. But this human sort of discovery can also become delightful. Besides, it's essential for The New Strong. Why?

Paying attention to yourself at human vibrational frequencies can inform you about that unique, precious, human identity of yours — the basis for using your full potential in life.

CHAPTER 16

How to Reboot Your Human Frequencies

Have you ever solved computer problems with a simple reboot? Our first skill set in this Program for Easy Vibrational Balance can give you a version of that. I'll help you align more strongly with human vibrational frequencies — which are related to the energies of The Great Mother, Mother Earth.

"Reboot Your Human Frequencies" can strengthen you greatly, both psychologically and spiritually. As a result you can expect to:

- Feel more comfortable in your body and surroundings.
- Enjoy a subtle peace of mind that underlies everyday experience.
- Benefit from a here-and-now emotional freshness.

Let's begin with the Teaching Version of this skill set. Please allow 30 minutes for the rest of this chapter and explore away. Subsequent use of this skill won't take nearly as long, because later you will be learning a Quick Version. For the instructions that come next, start clocking your Technique Time at Step #1. End it after you complete Step #9.

As usual, before you read more about this new skill set, please ask yourself, "Do I have that much Technique Time available now?"

If not, skip forward to Part Five and return later.

If your answer is yes, here we go: Woo-hoo!

Align with Mother Earth:
THE TEACHING VERSION

Mother Earth, now that's some body! Our planet has the largest physical body you're likely to meet, plus a consciousness all her own that can help you to value your humanity.

To prepare for alignment, choose a place outdoors where you can lie down undisturbed for as long as 20 minutes. A back yard might be perfect; maybe a park. Remember to bring along a timepiece, and maybe a towel or blanket.

For this alignment sequence it's preferable to lie on earth, not driveways or sidewalks. Just do your reasonable best, though. And if there is snow on the ground or it's rainy, you can always stay home and use the floor.

1. Lie on your belly, tucking in your chin until your forehead touches the ground. Name one thing out loud about how your body physically feels. Name one or more emotions. (This is the "Before" part of a "Before-and-After Picture.")

2. In the language of auras, body parts touching the earth will include most of your major CHAKRAS. In a playful way, notice how you happen to feel now energetically in these important energy centers: the base of your torso, your belly, ribcage, chest or breasts, forehead.

3. Your neck and the top of your head are also included in your set of major chakras. Feel them energetically but please don't contort your body to make them physically touch the ground, too. Easy does it.

4. Feel or imagine the presence of Mother Earth beneath you. Imagine or feel one chakra at a time being supported, connected to Her. Do this in a way that's enjoyable, of course. For instance, you might remember for a moment the delight that young children have enjoying their fresh, new, human-animal bodies.

5. In a playful way (not pushing yourself to do anything perfectly) notice your heartbeat. Your pulses. Your vibrational frequency.

6. Feel or imagine how Mother Earth also has a heartbeat. A pulse. A vibrational frequency.

7. Match yours to Hers. Pretend or explore, with the goal of feeling *Her* version in *your* body. If you like, request something like this out loud:

〰 *Dear precious body, shift my* **heartbeat** *to align with the heartbeat of Mother Earth.*

〰 *Shift my pulses to align with the* **pulses** *of Mother Earth.*

〰 *Shift my* **vibrational frequencies** *to align with the human vibrational frequencies of Mother Earth.*

8. Name one thing out loud about how your body physically feels. Name one or more emotions. (This is the "After" part of a "Before-and-After Picture.")

9. Out loud, thank your body. Thank Mother Earth. Then open your eyes.

Technique Time is over.

Just for fun, think about how you felt physically and emotionally. What was this like before you did the technique versus how you felt (and feel) afterwards? A human perspective, right?

Align with Mother Earth:
THE QUICK VERSION

No need to lie down for the Quick Version. You can do it standing up, whether outdoors or indoors. Say aloud:

Dear precious body, shift my heartbeat to align with the heartbeat of Mother Earth.

Shift my pulses to align with the pulses of Mother Earth.

Shift my vibrational frequencies to align with the human vibrational frequencies of Mother Earth."

That simple.

Of course there's more, much more to come. Your fun with skill sets for The New Strong is just beginning. Are you ready, beautifully rebooted you?

CHAPTER 17

Energy Shielding for The Age of Awakening

Despite all the training you've received since babyhood, human vibrational frequencies aren't the only game here at Earth School. You know about that, Powerfully Human Reader. But had you guessed this?

Every single day, astral happenings that concern you... far out-number all that occurs in human-level reality.

Even before the Age of Awakening this was true. Now it is more true than ever.

Did you ever turn your radio dial to find a station and mostly what you hear is static? All that extra astral activity on earth now — it sounds like static to your subconscious mind. Despite not being dangerous, it sure can feel distracting. (For many people this astral static is a cause of brain fog.)

Finding a Right-Sized Solution

In the Age of Awakening, with the veil gone, we humans deal with loads more astral static than before. It's reasonable to try to protect yourself with some kind of **ENERGY SHIELD**, but what kind?

My approach is like helping you to move your consciousness dial to the "station" that is your human identity, and then you can turn up the volume. This approach to shielding can protect you from being distracted by astral noise in the background.

I'll help you do that. Appropriately. Because what *don't* you need? A ridiculously elaborate kind of energy shield.

What's the point of going over-the-top-elaborate with shielding? From conversations I've had with clients, there are two main reasons.

#1. Fear

Static on the radio won't kill you, and neither will all that astral clutter. It's just an inconvenience, since everyone living now is naturally energy sensitive.

Fear not. In this chapter I'll help you to find a right-sized solution.

#2. Seeking a wrong kind of simple

Simple is good for an energy shield, yes. Not so good would be over-simplifying/exaggerating its protective value.

The veil is gone. No amount of energy shielding will bring it back. So what *can* a good shield do? Reduce energetic background noise, which is plenty.

And what *can't* a good shield do? Serve as a remedy for all 15 kinds of STUFF.

Powerfully Human Reader, it would be the wrong kind of simple to think, "Shields keep out all bad kinds of energy, especially those sinister neon-green potatoes."

This kind of misunderstanding leads to an all-too common practice today: energy shielding, off and on, all day long.

What you're learning here will help you as much as this sort of thing can. We're not trying to find an impossibly simple solution for all the many astral-level problems that *cannot* be solved with an energy shield.

Let's Right-Size This Type of Protection

"Your One-Minute Energy Shield" will be just big enough. For protection it will wake you up from within, aligning you better — like boosting your immune system by eating nutritious food.

Quite a different approach from the equivalent of dressing up with elbow-length gloves, a face mask, and old-fashioned chain mail.

Actually excessive shielding is worse than all that clunky gear. Aura reading shows that, technically, an energy shield is a THOUGHT FORM, an energetic structure added to the outside of a person's energy field.

Too thick or complicated a shield represents a problem, no matter how lovely that particular thought form might seem.

Why a problem? Let's use the example of Paige's routine for energetic shielding.

- She starts each day by visualizing a nice thick wad of golden light all around her, with mirrors attached on the outside to send other people's bad vibes back to them.
- Then Paige lovingly decorates her shield with affirmations galore.
- For extra security, she adds angels equipped with swords.
- And finally Paige speaks a series of affirmations that she is grounded, no matter what.
- What else? For the rest of her day, whenever Paige feels insecure (which is often) she repeats this performance.

So satisfying to her conscious mind!

Unfortunately, here's what happens at the subconscious and energetic level. The more Paige visualizes her shield, the better it works. Except it works to do *what*?

This is a gaudy, rigid thought form. And it's stuck partway through Paige's auric field.

Partway, you'll note. Powerfully Human Reader, a rigid thought form cannot always be larger than Paige's aura, since energy bodies are not made of molded plastic. All day long her aura (and yours) contracts and expands, depending upon innumerable factors.

For the protective purpose intended, might this rigid thought form be a problem? Well, hello!

To begin with, the shield so trustingly designed by Paige does not necessarily cover her entire aura, especially at those times when it naturally expands.

Picture a pair of elegant white gloves that seem to fit while getting dressed for the fancy dress ball. Only, in this analogy, the size of Paige's hands is variable. Frequently her hands protrude far beyond the boundaries of those dainty little gloves.

How great is the protective power of gloves (or a shield) when the body part being protected sticks out farther than the protective device itself?

Plus there's another problem.

Auric Modeling, For Better or Worse

Overdone energy shielding produces ugly results that are related to **AURIC MODELING**. Ironically hard-working people like Paige have no clue that what they're doing is so counter-productive.

What is auric modeling (besides inescapable)?

On a subconscious level, everyone reads auras. They're constantly on display, like the outfits worn by runway models in a fashion show.

What if you're talking to Emmett on the phone, or you're hanging out together in a room? Every single minute, you subconsciously notice his auric modeling. Same thing with every selfie he takes.

In every case, Emmett's aura is blabbing away nonstop... to the subconscious mind of every single bystander.

Granted, auric modeling does not register consciously. To get that knowledge consciously, develop skills of energetic literacy (which you definitely can).

Read auras to learn more about that weird thing you feel with Emmett, that something on the tip of your tongue; that is, at a subconscious level.

Powerfully Human Reader, regardless of whether you choose to spend Technique Time by purposely and consciously reading auras, what happens quite automatically?

Auric modeling constantly reveals what is going on with a person energetically. Happens with Emmett or Paige or you. Other people just know, in a vague way, what's up aurically.

Suppose that you're in the room with Paige. She might carry some dreadfully outdated facade bodies (the kind of STUFF you may have learned how to clean up from Book One of this series, "Use Your Power of Command for Spiritual Cleansing and Protection").

Sadly that STUFF sticks out like a sore thumb in Paige's auric modeling. Right there along with her bold, bright, overly elaborate energy shield.

Like it or not, every kind of STUFF in a person's aura shows completely. No energy shield will vanish this. Ever.

If Paige's energy shield cannot disguise her true auric modeling, what *does* it accomplish?

Adding to the rest of the auric mess, her shield reads like a big "Keep Out" sign. In no way does her shield serve as some type of privacy screen, so that others cannot read her aura. That's impossible.

But it can turn off people who otherwise might be interested in becoming her friends.

You see, astral-level frequencies are not simpler and stupider than human ones. It goes the other way around, actually.

- Using a shield to hide your auric modeling?
- Or to warn you about other people's energies?

⮑ Or to outsmart innumerable beings of astral frequency who might be nearby and can read your aura instantly?

Nice try!

No matter how elaborate Paige's attempt at shielding, it can never be as complex as her energy field. Because her aura includes up-to-date info on every chakra databank's current status; plus every bit of STUFF she carries now; plus memories of every single incident that has ever happened to Paige in her long history as a soul. And there's more, much more. You get the idea.

Therefore, elaborate energy shields are worse than useless for the protective purpose intended, plus they mess up auric modeling.

I've encountered this problem often, researching many a hard-working New Ager. Using energetic literacy, I'll find energetic shields, walls, and other unfortunate thought forms that folks who don't know better have installed for self-protection.

So well meant! Commendable, in theory. In practice? A bit pathetic.

By contrast, what will you get thanks to Your One-Minute Energy Shield? Better auric modeling will be produced, akin to improved muscle tone.

A flexible adornment of Divine frequency will be supplemented by a tiny (but effective) cleanup device that will impact you and you alone.

No unintended mixed messages. Nothing pathetic or astrally embarrassing. Just a little something nice.

Your One-Minute Energy Shield: EXPLORE THE TEACHING VERSION

For our Teaching Version, do the steps just as presented. Words in italics are to be spoken aloud.

Note: In your Before-and-After Picture I'll be referring to your left calf. Use this in Steps #2 and 9 unless you have soreness or pain in that part of your body; in which case, substitute a different body part that feels more normal.

1. Officially begin. Close your eyes. Name one or more emotions that you have right now. Open your eyes long enough to write this down, fast and sloppy, a.k.a. **SCRIBBLE-WRITING.**

2. Notice how your left calf feels physically now. Find some words to describe it; then open your eyes long enough to write this down with scribble-writing. Now your Before Picture is done. Open your eyes.

3. Stand up. Say, *I call upon you, God, to be here with me now as a super-charged presence.*

4. Take one deep breath (or Vibe-Raising Breath, if you have learned how to do that from Book One in this series).

5. *I awaken my Power of Command to co-create with you now.*

6. Close your eyes. Imagine/see/feel the energy field around you and pull it (inward or outward) until it's about 10 feet around you in every direction.

7. Open your eyes. *God, please place some gold and silver light around the edge of my aura, so that only energies that are 100% helpful for my human life may enter at any time.*

8. *On top of this add a generator violet flame. This will create more violet flames in a portable manner wherever I go. These flames will identify, then clean up, stale or negative energies... in my environment, food and drink, making them fresh, clear, clean, and recycled. Then add replacement energies to support the expression of my soul at my current level of development. Thank you.*

9. Repeat Steps 1 and 2. This will count as your After Picture.

10. Complete the technique. Eyes closed, think something like, "Now this technique is done." Then open your eyes.

Look over what you wrote in your Before-and-After Picture. Interesting?

Your One-Minute Energy Shield: RESULTS

Powerfully Human Reader, what did you notice?

Ideally you simply feel like yourself. Because this was a skill set for preventing problems, not self-healing. (Some tasty skills for that will come later.)

Feeling like yourself — that's a good thing. And for practical purposes, that's plenty.

It is not the job of an energy shield to turn you into somebody who notices energies all the time. Heaven forbid! You have the privilege of being human.

Which is not to say that you have just wasted your time with this powerfully protective new energy shield.

Your One-Minute Energy Shield: INSIDE INFORMATION

What can shielding protect you from, really?

Many kinds of STUFF are part of your aura and home. Some can be prevented, others healed; many you'll simply adjust to because you have basic mental health.

In this Age of Awakening, we need to be more sophisticated than before. It's very New Age to believe that an energy shield can magically fix everything.

That's like saying, "I will buy a magical bottle of soap. It will clean my laundry, my cooking utensils, every object in my home. If I have a cavity in my teeth, all I need do is gargle with my magical soap. If ever I'm feeling sick, I'll swallow a spoonful for an instant cure. By the way, this soap will also give me perfect skin."

Really?

We Post-New-Agers can understand that no one fancy protection works against every bad kind of energy. So I make more modest claims for your One-Minute Energy Shield. Installing it daily is like putting up a screen between your window and your living room.

With a physical screen, you can open that window wide and enjoy the fresh air. Mosquitoes and flies won't get through.

Similarly your One-Minute Energy Shield offers some protection against negative thought forms in the environment and other random forms of astral-level debris. A simple buffer, yet effective.

Your One-Minute Energy Shield: EVEN DEEPER INFORMATION

In the Age of Awakening, every human alive is dealing with a new degree of energy sensitivity. Understandably, many of us rely on one energy-related technique, over-using it like crazy — as in repeating it over and over, all day long.

I've known many well-meaning folks who were constantly shielding themselves or grounding their energies or tapping away or doing some other equivalent of "Magical Soap."

If a technique or skill set works, you don't have to do it all day long.

For best results with Your One-Minute Energy Shield, please, do it just once a day. Preferably in the morning. Your protection will last for 24 hours. That simple.

Your One-Minute Energy Shield QUICK VERSION

1. Stand up. *I call on you, God, to be here with me now as a super-charged presence.*

2. Take one deep breath or Vibe-Raising Breath.

3. *I awaken my Power of Command to co-create with you now."*

4. For two seconds, eyes open or closed, imagine your aura drawing inward or outward, until it's about 10 feet out from your body in every direction.

5. *God, please place around the edge of my aura some gold and silver light so that only energies that are 100% helpful for my human life may enter at any time.*

6. *On top of this add a generator violet flame. This will create more violet flames in a portable manner in my environment, food, and drink; always cleaning up stale or negative energies; making them fresh, clear, clean and recycled.*

7. *Then add replacement energies that support the expression of my soul. Thank you."*

CHAPTER 18

Just Two Minutes More For Mega-Protection

In this Age of Awakening certain energy problems involve energetic flows between other people and you. If a stranger looks down on you (literally), that can temporarily weaken your aura.

Other energetic flows occur between you and astral-level "people." Say that you walk into a convenience store and, unbeknownst to your conscious mind, a bunch of stuck spirits look you over. That can also weaken your aura temporarily.

To keep either type of energy flow from becoming a nuisance, it's smart to do something. But how big a something?

Granted, we're talking casual encounters here.

Casual, compared to what?

Suppose that you have stuck spirits, or ghosts, habitually attached to the outside of your aura. They're not just looking you over, fun as usual while observing the human parade at the 7-Eleven.

These stuck spirits would not be a casual energetic flow but, rather, a different problem, one that can be pretty simple to fix. Book One of this series teaches you how to co-create a healing that will permanently relocate those stuck spirits off-planet. A true win-win!

But casual encounters with astral beings at the 7-Eleven are different, right? Powerfully Human Reader, it would be more than a full-time job for you to clean up random astral entities everywhere you go, trying to prevent them from looking you over.

Same goes for consciously plumping up your energy field every time some random human stranger gives you a dirty look. Which is why you can benefit from the skill set in this chapter.

I'm going to teach you a simple solution to random, draining energy flows with other people. This highly effective two-minute method is called "LOCK THE DOOR AND HIDE THE KEY."

Locking the door to your home — that's no big ordeal, is it? An equally simple routine can provide a decent amount of protection from random energy drains.

Lock the Door and Hide the Key:
TEACHING VERSION

Such an undemanding routine, how long will it take? Two minutes or less per day. How hard can a skill be if you can do it that fast?

Learning properly will take us a bit longer, of course, but after doing our Teaching Version once? You'll progress to the Quick Version.

Lock the Door and Hide the Key:
PRACTICE THE POSITION

Your energy system can be understood in many ways. Starting thousands of years ago, Traditional Chinese Medicine discovered 12 invisible channels that distribute life force energy within the human body. These are called **MERIDIANS**.

Many mind-body-spirit modalities make use of this knowledge: most famously, acupuncture; other systems include shiatsu, acupressure, Touch for Health, Eden Energy Medicine, The Body Code System.

Two of these meridians will be used for "Lock the Door and Hide the Key."

Your **CENTRAL MERIDIAN** lies in front of your body. It runs from your pubic bone up to your *lower* lip.

For this skill of energy protection, think of a line that starts where your legs meet, goes up your body, and ends at the center of your lower lip.

Your **GOVERNING MERIDIAN** starts at your tailbone, moves up your spine, wraps over your head and ends at the center of your *upper* lip.

For this skill of energy protection, we'll focus on a portion of this meridian, moving backwards — all that's needed for our purposes: from your forehead, over your head, and down to the prominent bone at the base of your neck.

Powerfully Human Reader, when doing this skill set for self-protection, you will be brushing a few fingertips of one hand lightly over a portion of each of these meridians.

If you like, you could use your second hand, too. Placing that hand on top of your other one might feel supportive and extra-balanced. (Personally I prefer doing that.)

Chiropractor Bradley Nelson, founder of The Body Code System, has a great idea for intensifying the effect of brushing the meridians of your electromagnetic field. You can use a small kitchen magnet to help protect your electromagnetic energies.

If you want to try that, hold the magnet so its magnetic surface makes contact with your body or whatever clothes you're wearing. Why keep your clothes on? Because this skill set is called "Lock the Doors, Hide the Key" not "Strip and Search Yourself."

Either way, brushing a meridian is done lightly, like using a paintbrush to apply watercolors.

Practice the Two Positions

1. The Energy Line

Here's how to practice "Lock the Door" Position #1. At the bottom of your torso, middle of your body, place your fingertips where the legs come together.

Brush up the center all the way to the middle of your lower lip. Then release your touch.

Make this movement like a quick brushstroke of protection. Practice a few times until this is quick and comfortable for you. From now on, I'll call it "THE ENERGY LINE."

2. The Coat Hanger

"Lock the Door" Position #2 is a brushstroke shaped like the top of a coat hanger. Or you might picture it like the top of a question mark, wrapping around your head.

Place your fingertips at your forehead, just above your eyebrows. Brush upwards, passing your hairline, then across the top of your head and down your neck. Stop at the big bone that lies at the base of your neck. Technically that's your Seventh Cervical Vertebra, C7.

Practice this brushstroke movement a few times until you find it quick and comfortable. From now on, I'll call it "THE COAT HANGER."

Lock the Door and Hide the Key:
EXPLORE THE TEACHING VERSION

Eight steps are needed for this skill set. For our Teaching Version only, I will ask you to add some extra before-and-after.

Please read through the following steps, then do them just as presented. For most of these steps your eyes will be closed. To find out what the next step will be, open your eyes to take a peek at your instructions, then close eyes again and continue.

Note: I'll be referring to your left shoulder. Use this in Steps #3 and 7 unless you find soreness or pain in that part of your body (in which case, substitute a different body part that feels more normal).

1. Think, "Technique begins."

2. Close your eyes. Name one or more emotions that you have right now. Open your eyes long enough to write it down, fast and sloppy — scribble-writing.

3. Notice how your left shoulder feels physically right now. Find some words to describe that. Open your eyes long enough to write this down with scribble-writing. And now your Before Picture is done!

4. Combine the first physical movement with words. You have already practiced this movement, The Energy Line. So use your paintbrush of protection, brushing a line straight up your torso all the way to your lower lip.
    Words to Accompany: As you do the movement say, *I am safe and balanced.*
    Repeat the combo of movement and words until you have done it three times.

5. Combine the second physical movement with words. You have already practiced this movement, The Coat Hanger. Start low on your forehead, then go straight up over your forehead, curving around your head, and include that prominent bone at the base of your neck.
    Words to Accompany: As you do the movement say, *I'm protected from negative energy flows with other people.*
    Brush and speak the words... three times in a row.

6. Once again, you will combine a physical movement with words. In this case you won't be using either of the two motions you've practiced. Instead I'm going to describe for you the way to do the "Lock the Door" part of this skill set.

(You may remember, the name for this complete skill set is "Lock the Door and Hide the Key.)

To "Lock the Door," each time you use this skill set you will choose one random body part to anchor in your protection and activate it.

For this particular time, make one choice. (Each morning from now on, when using this skill set, you can choose somewhere different from the day before.)

Varying locations will keep your practice fresh each day. Of course, there are limits. You only have so many body parts to choose from, so don't worry about repeating these locations over time. Place your palm on the location you've selected for today, such as your right knee, your navel, or your left shin.

As you say the following words, imagine that you are activating your protection, then hiding the mechanism deep within you. Imagine a movement like turning a key in a lock.

Words to Accompany: As you do this movement, say *Protect me, God.* (Substitute, if desired, the name of a different Divine Being. Just don't substitute the name of a favorite celebrity, dead relative, astral being, etc.)

7. Repeat Steps 2 and 3. This will count as your After Picture.

8. Finish up. Eyes closed, think something like, "Now this technique is done. And I did great!" Open your eyes.

Lock The Door and Hide the Key: RESULTS

What did you notice? This skill set protects your auric field from being bombarded by astral energies from other people. Results are subtle, due to STUFF *not* entering your aura.

Non-drama is what you want in a form of prevention, right? Though gentle, some immediate results may still have shown in your Before-and-After Picture. So compare what you wrote down.

Did you wind up feeling a bit more like yourself? That could mean feeling more confident, resourceful, awake, more full of life (in short, more strongly positioned in human frequencies).

Of course, the biggest results lie in what you *don't* feel, especially many hours later.

Interested in Extra Protection?

Before sleep, say aloud three times, "*Protect me, God.*" This reboots your vibrational resourcefulness during sleep and dreaming. So you may fall asleep more easily, sleep more soundly, and wake up just a bit more refreshed.

Lock The Door and Hide the Key: INSIDE INFORMATION

1. Less energetic clutter

Other people share this world with you. (Hope you don't mind.) Astral interactions happen constantly, with energies moving back and forth between you and others. With less subconscious-level clutter, you may take more of an interest in life, your life.

As a result, you may be less distracted by random energies moving in and out of your aura.

2. A stronger sense of identity

With "Lock the Door, Hide the Key," you can feel more secure as a person. Not like superpowers. More like having normal balance while you walk, and expecting that you can walk through life just fine.

Human life only appears to be all that is happening here at Earth School. So many astral interactions take place.

By minimizing ones that distract or confuse you subconsciously, your sense of self will grow stronger. So take heart, Powerfully Human Reader.

3. Triple protection vibrationally

Is it just coincidence?

- Each movement is made three times.
- Each set of healing words is spoken three times.

Coincidence? Ha! Three is a powerful number for energy healing skills like this one. Human, astral, and Divine — each of these three levels within you is awakened when you "Lock the Door, Hide the Key."

Just remember, say all three reps out loud. Never just think them mentally.

Speaking allows sound waves to be produced, human-level sound waves. You become a broadcaster, even if nobody hired you to host a radio show.

Powerfully Human Reader, thanks to this part of your new skill set, guess what? You're broadcasting the truth of your human identity into all three different realms.

4. Which words?

"I am safe and balanced" brings protection and balance to your auric field, as it is right now.

These words add power to the functioning of your Central Meridian. Next you bolster the impact with backwards brushing of your Governing Meridian while saying, "I'm protected from negative energy flows with other people."

This combo prevents negative flows of energy with other human beings and also opportunistic astral beings. Additional help with the latter will follow in later chapters; still it's wise to start with prevention.

More About How That Extra Protection Works

Have you tried it yet, Powerfully Human Reader? I mean the optional Extra Protection with "Lock the Door and Hide the Key."

This provides extra protection during sleep and dreaming, states of awareness where your consciousness is not primarily involved with human vibrational frequencies.

While your physical body rests and recharges, awareness travels by identifying with one or more of your energy bodies, having fabulous adventures as a superhero. Or whatever else you're doing in the various dream worlds.

If ever you needed evidence that so-called "Human" life isn't mostly about being human, think about sleep and dreaming. Deprived of those out-of-physical-body excursions, what would happen to you after several days? You would be dead.

Fortunately, you're very much alive. For that reason, it's useful to awaken vibrational protection while setting out on your mysterious sleep-time adventures.

QUICK VERSION: Lock the Door and Hide the Key

1. Close your eyes. Notice something about yourself as a human being, such as a physical sensation or an emotion. Open your eyes.

2. Three times, up The Energy Line. Say each time, *I am safe and balanced.*

3. Three times, down The Coat Hanger. Say each time, *I'm protected from negative energy flows with other people.*

4. Choose one body part to anchor in your protection and activate it. Using this skill set each morning, choose somewhere different from the day before. Lock the door and hide the key. Say, *Protect me, God.*

5. Optional: Before sleep, say once out loud, *Protect me, God.* This reboots your vibrational resourcefulness during sleep and dreaming.

CHAPTER 19

Transitional Vibrational Challenges

Living The New Strong will be different for generations to come. Powerfully Human Reader, you're among the first group of human beings to experience life in this Age of Awakening.

Exciting though this is — a great privilege, really — certain problems arise related to the sheer newness. As a consequence, we need to adapt in a way that future generations won't even be able to imagine.

Of course, that's why you have been told about today's new vibrational rules. Twenty or even ten years from now, these rules will have gone mainstream. Instead of being "new rules," they will have become, for most people, simply "the values we live by."

Our whole Program for Easy Vibrational Balance exists to help you grow faster by learning how to take advantage of great opportunities, newly available, during the world's transition into Post-New-Age life.

In all the universe, earth is now special. It's rare for an incarnational world to make such a huge transition. Unfortunately, some astral beings are trying to get a piece of the action. I think of the resulting problems as temporary and transitional.

Ever Hear of the Carpetbaggers?

Once upon a time, in America, some people were challenged by a comparable group of opportunistic beings, only these ones were human. They caused problems right after the Civil War.

After the slaves had been freed, the carpetbaggers moved in. These unscrupulous scoundrels saw an opportunity to take advantage of people caught in transition.

What, you've never heard of the carpetbaggers? Google them and you can learn about their sad little blip in American history.

Why don't people today talk much about carpetbaggers, or fear them? Opportunistic behavior like that can work for a while. It lasts only until smart people learn better than to let themselves be influenced.

At Earth School today, we have a comparable problem. Only today's carpetbaggers are astral beings, opportunistic entities.

Powerfully Human Reader, in this chapter I'll introduce you to these astral beings as they used to visit earth before the Age of Awakening.

Next chapter I'll describe how some of these beings have turned opportunistic, their version of becoming carpetbaggers. And I'll teach you a skill set that will solve problems that they're causing.

Personally, I'm convinced that all this is temporary. As more people adjust to earth's vibrational transition, and follow the new rules for this age, we'll be done for good with these astral carpetbaggers. First, though, we must actively avoid this sort of problem.

Although this time of transition will be over eventually, that doesn't mean all you can do now is to passively wait. Let's get going. I'm preparing you to learn another easy-to-use skill set. It works just fine, no fuss and no worries. We'll start with a basic definition.

What Is an ET?

An **ET**, or **EXTRATERRESTRIAL BIOLOGICAL ENTITY**, is a person like you or me. Except with some pretty big differences:

~ No ET was *born on earth with a human body.* (You and I have had that privilege. Quite some privilege! Especially to rate an incarnation now, during that growthful time of the Shift into The Age of Awakening.)

- No ET was born *anywhere* on earth, including the U.S.A. Therefore, not eligible to become a president of the United States. (Joke. Although also true.)

- Every ET has incarnated on *another world*. (If you think Earth School is the only planet supporting intelligent life, think again. Though it's tough, we do evolve ultra-fast here. Besides, rumor has it, we serve the best food.)

- Using regular human-level perception, you can't hear or see ETs. They are perceived with awareness at an astral level. (And perceiving them is not required at all for you to succeed at the self-healing skill set that I'll be teaching you.)

- Many different kinds of ETs are targeted in our upcoming skill set. What do they have in common? Each one was born in a world advanced enough to achieve transport to this world. (Whether "Beam me up, Scotty" or the spaceship kind of travel.)

- And each ET relevant to our discussion has *chosen* to come to earth. (Why? More on that soon.)

For generations, ETs have visited earth. You may have seen a delightful movie that was made about this, "ET: The Extra-Terrestrial."

You may be a Trekkie or go to Comic-Con. You may be a believer in alien abductions. Or, maybe, no thanks. Preferences like these lie outside the scope of this Program for Easy Vibrational Balance. Here our purpose is practical.

Powerfully Human Reader, skeptical or not, it's in your interest to learn a bit more about ETs. So here come seven practical points:

1. An ET is different from a **GHOST** or **STUCK SPIRIT** that could get attached to the outside of your aura. (You can learn how to get them off, and also free them up, with a skill set from Book One in this series for Energy HEALING Skills.)

2. An ET is different from an **ASTRAL ENTITY**, like your wonderful Grandma Gisela, who died when you were a teenager. Since then she has taken up residence in a very lovely heaven. And, yes, you could now literally call her "an angel."

3. ETs from different words are *not all the same,* just as you would expect certain differences from a New Yorker versus a native of Tokyo or Timbuktu. Some ETs can be trusted more than others, but you are not required to trust any of them particularly because they are astral beings and, as such, are none of your business.

4. ETs are individuals, with access to free will just like you. Because all of us girls and boys who grew up in New York City (like me) are hardly identical: same deal with ETs, only more so.

5. ETs live at an astral frequency. Which one? Depends on which world they come from. Whichever, it wasn't earth. So no ET knows the value of being mortal as you do, Powerfully Human Reader.

6. Astral vibrational frequencies are higher than those on earth. In some ways any ET tourist knows more than you do.

    But they sure don't know better than you about living on earth. Like how to be happy here. Or what will help you, personally, as an evolving human being.
    We biped earthlings have home turf wisdom, plus sovereignty over our auras. That you can trust!

7. Just because ETs have higher vibrations than humans doesn't mean they bring the balance, judgment, or spiritual radiance of Divine Beings.

    With all respect, they don't. They are merely astral beings, evolving towards Enlightenment but not there yet. Just like most human beings living on earth today!
    No need to idolize ETs because they can travel to other worlds in a way you cannot; they are simply having a different kind of incarnation.

Actually the sort of ET who gets involved with people here these days... may be far less evolved than you.

Why ETs USED TO Get Stuck Here

During the New Age years, I had good teachers for learning about ET entities. Why might they get stuck to the outside of a person's aura? How could I facilitate self-healing energetically?

My teachers were Rev. AlixSandra Parness and Rev. Rich Bell, ministers with Teaching of the Inner Christ (TIC). After Sandi promoted me to Lay Minister, I began using the self-healing skills I'd been taught, skills that I later adapted for RES. (To learn more about the generous help I received from the TIC organization, see Book One in this series on Energy HEALING Skills for the Age of Awakening.)

Let me give you a summary of what I learned about extraterrestrials back then. (Yowza, 30 years ago!)

ETs are non-human beings who live in other worlds. Sometimes they come to earth as tourists. Earth can be a fascinating place to visit. We have such powerful illusions, including emotions like fear, sadness, and anger.

ETs come to observe us humans, watching us handle these ever-changing emotions — plus all the other challenges of daily life — just as we might watch a TV show about an athlete training for a big race. Courageous! Exotic! So different from regular life back home!

Unfortunately some of those tourists wind up getting stuck during their trip. What happens then? It isn't like the movie "ET: The Extra-Terrestrial," where the spaceship took off and cute little ET got left behind by accident, and then he phoned home to get rescued.

What really happens? Many ET tourists are not nearly as ready as they think. They struggle to stay balanced when dealing with

human life. Despite being briefed intellectually, they aren't prepared experientially. So earth's heavy illusions can clobber them.

Compare that to your everyday life, Powerfully Human Reader.
Even on a bad day, you handle earth's illusions pretty darned well:
You may not welcome emotions like fear, anger, loneliness, and
sadness. Yet they don't weird you out as something totally alien.

As discussed in Part One of this book, you were raised to believe
in these illusions. By adulthood you had gained a working knowledge about how to deal with them.

For us, involvement in human life isn't some tourist trip gone awry
but the whole point. To evolve here as a person, with normal mental health, we need to feel human emotions, to care a great deal
about physical survival, and so forth.

Understandably many an unsuspecting ET tourist is seduced by
our heavy vibrations. They can get caught up in beliefs like a
popular one here: supposedly we can't feel good unless we fit in
with lots of other human-type people.

Uh-oh!

These heavy illusions could be harder for a tourist to handle than
for us. By way of analogy, say that Rahul is born in Calcutta, India.
He grows up drinking the water, handling the various critters in
it, developing immunity to them. By adulthood, he doesn't need to
boil the water, does he?

By contrast, Randy is born in Chicago, and he's perfectly healthy
while living in America. Traveling to India has been his dream, so
at age 42 he goes and has a great time.

But oh boy, afterwards does he ever get sick! Parasites are Randy's
unplanned souvenir, since he never grew up drinking that water.

Sure, eventually Randy can get his health back. But here's the
point. When Randy romanticized going to India, parasites were
not on his bucket list.

Likewise many ETs come to earth because visiting us seems wonderful. Then they get more than they bargained for.

Sometimes Earth School looks as gorgeous as the Taj Mahal; other times, it might seem more like Alcatraz. Therefore, many ETs forget who they are.

Reduced to a semi-snooze, not only can't they phone home. Some barely remember there *is* a home beyond this heavy-vibed place of never-ending drama.

When these ETs attach to the outside of people's auras, it helps the psychic-level beings calm down. But how great is it for the human involved?

That arrangement wasn't made with conscious consent. And it's really not such a great deal for humans, having these astral beings located up close and personal. ETs automatically produce an astral influence that subtly detracts from a human's natural vibrational alignment.

Which is why, in our next chapter, you'll be given energy healing skills to efficiently clean up your aura, even while helping those ETs to awaken and move on to their next right place of expression.

All this is reason enough to learn our next skill set. However there's more to the story, now that we're living in the Age of Awakening.

Why So Many ETs Come Here NOW

Decades ago what I learned about ETs was plenty for practical purposes. But historically what followed? A period of accelerated vibrational quickening nudged our planet forward, culminating in the Shift into the Age of Awakening.

With the veil gone, humans like us are changing rapidly, adjusting to our new energy sensitivity. Even if most of us haven't learned yet about that veil-less-ness, don't you think that ETs will have noticed it? And noticed it very clearly?

Of course! Not only do ETs have higher-vibe bodies compared to ours. Like all astral beings, and unlike most humans, automatically they can read auras fluently.

Powerfully Human Reader, no matter where you were born and raised, your mother tongue is human *objective* reality. For example, this was my son's first sentence:

"Holly. Swing. Uh-oh." (Translation? His friend Holly sat on a swing at the playground. Then she fell off.)

As we grow up, kids also learn to speak surface-level *subjective* reality. Like "I think you are sooooo cute, Holly."

Reaching adulthood, we speak Human fluently. Some of us do choose to get extra skills and learn the "second language" of energetic literacy. Regardless, each of us speaks, thinks, and feels in the primary language of Human.

By contrast, what is the primary language for an ET who is visiting earth? Energetic literacy may be the first language. Otherwise, depending on where that ET has been living, maybe that energy talk becomes the second language. Either way, energy reading is totally fluent. While, lacking our peculiarly low-vibrational bodies, ETs cannot fully speak Human. Ever.

Yet they definitely have good reason to flock here now. In Earth's Age of Awakening, a rare astral show occurs daily. How often does *any world* have their version of the veil disappear? Maybe once every 40,000 years? Not often, that's for sure.

Since earth's vibrational rules have begun to change, every human is adjusting one way or another. How much fun that must be to watch, since our auras reveal what we go through day by day.

The Greatest Show on Earth Is... Earth

Of course, this planet has always been rich in drama. Since the Shift, the amount of astral-level drama has only increased.

Many of us have become vulnerable vibrationally, playing with energy like a shiny new toy. We're actively seeking spiritual answers (which is good), but most are doing this without discernment (which brings trouble).

Good or bad, from an ET's perspective, this is quite the rare treat to observe.

To them, we post-Shift earthlings have tremendous psychic sex appeal. And so the visitors now come in droves.

Newly arrived at our Post-New-Age planet, these tourists start off functioning normally. Yet soon the heavy illusions of earth can seduce them, as has happened historically with many ETs, until they are dumbed down by our anger, fear, sadness, and the rest of the planet's heavy illusions.

Between unfamiliar emotional drama and our uniquely dense vibrational frequencies, earth experience confuses many of these ET tourists. And now, adding to the confusion, human consciousness displays the wild new fluidity of No More Veil.

This dynamic only intensifies how ETs can get stuck. Besides that, others are coming now for an altogether different reason.

The Astral Carpetbaggers

Mostly I call them OPPORTUNISTIC EXTRATERRESTRIAL ENTITIES, because they're seeking influence over us. Could be idealism or maybe something more cynical, depending upon the entity. Regardless, influence is possible now in ways that it wasn't before. And you know why, right?

So many of us are playing with energies, remember? Yet without discernment.

Playing with that shiny new toy, it is so tempting to seek out special messages, channelings, even energetic attunements.

ETs may seem to possess special wisdom, yet how often is it truthfully labeled as "The Romance of the Astral"?

While it's true that ETs live at higher frequencies, they don't necessarily have our best interests at heart. Even when well intended:

- ～ They do not have human bodies that were given to them by God for the purpose of spiritual evolution.
- ～ They cannot speak Human or otherwise understand life from a human vantage point.
- ～ And they are not necessarily more evolved spiritually than people like you or me, who were accorded the privilege of evolving here at Earth School at this extraordinary time in history.

As I've learned from helping clients, today many ETs are aiming to strongly influence people, turning them away from interest in "ordinary" life until they become willing associates, even puppets.

Other ETs are just having fun, acting like eavesdroppers while stuck to a person's aura, vicariously observing what we do (without our conscious knowledge or consent).

Wouldn't you rather be your own person, self-directed, and taking full advantage of your chance to evolve super-fast here at Earth School?

Evolution slows down considerably when lots of ETs get stuck to your energy field or live in your home. So here's the big question. What can you do about that?

CHAPTER 20

Helping ETs to Phone Home
And Go Home

Does it seem ironic to you, Powerfully Human Reader? ETs are awake enough to hitchhike, or otherwise travel through space, in order to arrive at Earth. Yet their one-time awakeness does not really help you one bit.

Some ETs have become confused while here, whereas others have turned downright opportunistic, aiming to influence us humans as though we needed them... for our personal growth.

What nonsense! Your human life belongs to you, *supported* by astral vibrational energies but not *dominated* by them, not unless you allow that.

Back in Chapter 8, you were introduced to your Personal Angel Team, assigned to you before birth, helping to keep you safe energetically. This includes your guardian angel plus a couple of spirit guides. As life progresses, your Personal Angel Team will naturally expand to include more astral entities as appropriate.

These helpers are Divinely approved. How do they help you, exactly? When advice is needed, your Personal Angel Team whispers into your subconscious mind.

Otherwise leadership is yours. Using free will, you're responsible for choosing what makes you humanly happy, overcoming problems, helping others. All this is how humans evolve here at Earth School.

So long as your Personal Angel Team works normally, random astral beings can't join your team. Without your having to do a thing, you're protected in that way.

What's different now in this Age of Awakening? With the veil gone, opportunistic ETs can crash the party. They can influence you even if they're never included officially as a member of your Personal Angel Team.

Why might you become a person of interest to these ETs? If you seek guidance from "spirit," if you're partial to channeled information, or if you believe that psychic-level advisors have wisdom superior to your own, oops!

Well, you can stop that right now. Use human discernment to prevent problems with ETs.

1. Don't believe psychics who call you "Supremely gifted," or promise that you're being taught ultimate wisdom, or feed you similar vanity nonsense.

2. Please, avoid calling on "spirit" as if it means God. It doesn't. Plenty of opportunistic astral beings are spirits. Sadly, a trusting request for help from "spirit" will probably summon one of them.

3. As a consumer, ask where a healing is sourced. Some *energy healing professionals* have skills for working along with God, rather than astral spirits. Say "Yes" to Divine co-creation and "No" to assistance from astral beings or "spirit."

4. *You* can develop skills to co-create with God. That includes what you're learning to do in this chapter!

5. Especially avoid receiving spiritual initiations or attunements. In the Age of Awakening this can result in allowing ETs to become deeply enmeshed with your energy field.

All that's prevention. Now let's bring on the healing.

Yes, You Can Free Yourself from ETs

"Which extraterrestrial entities do I have? Are they from Mars or from Venus?"

Who knows just how many types of ETs exist in all the universe?

Here's what I do know:

- When ETs get stuck in *this* world, their bodies are made of energy at relatively high-vibe astral frequencies.
- And the method you are about to learn will get them unstuck from your aura.

ET Entity Healing: PREPARE TO LEARN

Powerfully Human Reader, this upcoming skill set is complex. It contains more steps than the other skills you've learned so far. Yet every step will make sense. Now I'm about to prepare you systematically before you even start learning the specifics of our latest skill set.

Pretty exciting, really! You're learning a super-efficient way to move out dozens or hundreds or even thousands of ET entities.

What a privilege it is to facilitate a healing like this — yet you won't have to prepare for years, poring over interstellar maps or mastering astrophysics.

Although some ETs can be amazingly evolved, your everyday state of awareness as a human being is plenty. To facilitate this energy healing, just do all the steps as I teach them to you, skipping nothing and adding nothing.

Go ahead. If you like, take a moment to gloat in advance.

Here you are, someone who previously may not have known how to effectively heal the tiniest bit of astral-level debris. And now you're exquisitely shielded, benefitting from superb positioning of consciousness... and becoming a hotshot interstellar healer.

Something New When You Co-Create this Healing

Of course you're going to co-create with Divine-level help. To successfully move out ETs stuck to the outside of your aura, it's essential to team up with a Divine Being in a body.

Compared to what? "In a body" does not mean the omnipresent, omnipotent, twinkling presence of the Divine, which is how we have co-created so far. Technically, that magnificent presence is the IMPERSONAL ASPECT of God.

Each time you facilitate the ET Healing, choose a PERSONAL ASPECT of the Divine, like one of these:

- An ASCENDED MASTER, a Divine-level being in a body, either associated with a world religion (like Jesus, Buddha, Kwan Yin) or revered as a god or goddess (like Isis, Athena, Apollo) or a deceased spiritual teacher who attained Enlightenment while on earth (like Merlin, St. Germain).

- Alternatively you might select an ARCHANGEL, another kind of Divine Being in a body. Archangels (like Archangel Michael, Archangel Gabriel, or Archangel Raphael) are more evolved than astral-level angels.

Maybe you're wondering, Powerfully Human Reader: why *not* facilitate this healing with the impersonal aspect of God?

Well, imagine that you have fallen asleep on a train and are being awakened by somebody who is helping you to safely return home. Which would you prefer, a person in a body or a twinkling, shining presence of majesty without any specific body at all?

(For a fuller discussion of Divine Beings, see Book One in this series of Energy HEALING Skills for the Age of Awakening.)

ET HEALING: Explore the Teaching Version

This skill set includes three parts. Promise me this, Powerfully Human Reader. Whenever you do this energy healing, always complete all three parts.

No matter which exotic Earth neighborhood you hail from —
even Brooklyn, with its wonderful subways — your results from
this healing will be superb. But only if you complete the full healing. Otherwise, you'll waste everyone's time. Since ETs may not
function in what we humans call "Time," wouldn't that be ironic!

PART ONE, ET HEALING. Educate and Release the ETs

Close your eyes. Notice how it feels to be you right now. How do
you feel physically, emotionally, and/or mentally? Put words to
the experience. It's *your* Before Picture. Write this down, fast and
sloppy — scribble-writing.

Open your eyes. Say out loud what follows in italics. (In this procedure I will give the example of Archangel Gabriel, but feel free to
substitute the name of a different Ascended Master or Archangel.)

*Archangel Gabriel, I call upon you to be here with me now in your
Universal Cosmic Divine body of light. I awaken my Power of
Command to co-create with you now. Place golden light around
my aura and the place where I am now, so that only energies that
are 100% helpful for my human life may enter at any time.*

*All you extraterrestrial beings, Dear Ones, I am speaking to each
of you personally, along with Archangel Gabriel. Hello. And congratulations. This is a healing ceremony just for you. Soon you
will be relocated to your next, perfect place of expression. I am so
happy to be able to help you.*

*Relax and receive this healing. You are safe. You are going to feel
so much better soon.* [Repeat for 30 seconds.]

*Here are three gifts for you. Take at least a little bit of each one.
Take even more if you wish:*

*Gift #1 is Universal Cosmic Divine LOVE. You deserve this
because of who you are deep down.*

Gift #2 is Universal Cosmic Divine TRUTH. Now you can recognize who you are and where you are. Before you were stuck. Now things are going to change for the better.

Gift #3 is Universal Cosmic Divine LIGHT. Aren't things becoming clearer now? Although you are here on earth, your body does not belong here. Wake up and notice where you are.

You are becoming free from fear and pain and everything else about earth's vibrations. You're free in this dimension and all other dimensions.

Now Archangel Gabriel is going to escort you personally to your next place of development, the place that is right for you. Go in peace.

PART TWO, ET HEALING: Put in appropriate energies

Say out loud:

I call on Archangel Gabriel to fill this place and me with Universal Cosmic Divine Love, Universal Cosmic Divine Truth, and Universal Cosmic Divine Light.

I close off my aura so that only energies that are 100% helpful for my human life may enter at any time.

PART THREE. ET HEALING. Complete the healing.

Say out loud:

Archangel Gabriel, please give me a multi-dimensional healing of astral ties. Find every astral tie between me and every ET entity involved with this healing, plus everyone I know in this world.

Please cut and dissolve all these astral ties, in every dimension.

Then fill us with new love and light and peace.

Thank you, Archangel Gabriel. It is done. It is done. It is done.

Now for your After Picture, Powerfully Human Reader. Close your eyes. Notice how it feels to be you right now. How do you feel physically, emotionally, and/or mentally? Put words to the experience. It's *your* After Picture. Write this down, fast and sloppy — scribble-writing.

Open your eyes.

Complete the technique. Eyes closed, think something like, "Now this technique is done." Open your eyes.

ET HEALING: Results

Well, give yourself a cosmic, multi-dimensional round of applause! Okay, that's a brain teaser. Cosmic, multi-dimensional applause could be even harder to visualize than the sound of one hand clapping. Regular old two-handed human clapping would be just fine.

Even that isn't needed unless you feel like it. If you followed the procedure, you have done this healing successfully. Do you notice some gentle improvement now? Feeling more like yourself!

Improvements may also have shown up in your Before-And-After comparison. Review that scribble-writing you did. Assess. Applaud to taste.

Maybe you've noticed a lot, maybe not so much. Your biggest results will come later, when everyday situations produce normal negative emotions like anger, fear, or loneliness.

Now those emotions may not grow as intense, nor stay with you as long. After all, you have just removed the equivalent of an echo chamber for negativity that used to be attached to your aura.

ET HEALING:
More About How This Technique Helps You

Last time you went to the pet shop, here's what you didn't buy. A visitor from another world, some random space tourist, anxiously confused. Or pushy and opportunistic. (At least I'm pretty sure you never went shopping for that.)

Would you have taken this home, either as a pet or a permanent roommate? Definitely not! Really, how would you have responded if such a being had asked you in human words:

"Is it okay if I stick to the outside of your aura? Maybe hang out in your bedroom? It's the best I can figure out, given how lost I feel. True, I will drain your energy slightly and cause minor but annoying problems in everyday life. Still, I'm feeling so needy. It's okay with you, right?"

Ugh! Several human-level problems can be solved due to the energetic decluttering you have just given yourself.

1. Vague discontent, vanished

ETs stuck to your aura could have caused you to feel vaguely "off." Maybe even contributed to spiritual addiction or psychological overwork.

Underlying fears may have crept in. Because astral junk doesn't feel comfortable to the kind of people who aim for The New Strong.

Here's my advice, Powerfully Human Reader. For the next week or so, notice occasionally how it feels to be you. Just a second or two of noticing, *not* in a big-deal, deep, Technique Time-kind of way.

Do you feel like yourself? Are you feeling alive and interested in live? Positive answers aren't flashy. They're normal and natural. You know, human.

2. Avoid appearing to others like a space case

With 100 or more ETs stuck to your aura, problems escalate in direct proportion to the number of astral hitchhikers. With even more ETs, the positioning of your consciousness could have been affected, skewing towards astral.

Thus you could have become spaced out or accident prone, even having what I call ASTRAL STINK in your auric modeling.

Astral stink means that your auric modeling includes the presence of astral components that are not YOU. To my perception, it's as annoying as the sound of fingernails scraping against a blackboard.

This distinctive, high-pitched squeak makes me uncomfortable. And, yes, in a subtle way it smells bad, too.

Just my personal imagery. But there's a comparable feeling of discomfort for most people who subconsciously encounter this astral presence.

Wouldn't it be nice to clean up this cause of astral stink? That, of course, is what you're learning how to do now.

3. Diminish any spacey withdrawal from human life

Depending on the number of ETs stuck to your energy field, certain human-level problems could have developed or been made worse, such as:

- Trying to escape everyday problems with energetic get-rich-quick schemes.
- Reluctance to solve human-type problems, lack of persistence.
- Procrastination.
- Finding it hard to connect to other people.
- Or to work.
- Or to accomplish much of anything.
- Being attracted to spiritual paths that exacerbate spacey detachment.

And, of course, ETs stuck to your aura can intensify any tendency toward addiction, involving either drink, drugs, candy, pornography, or even smoking cigarettes.

So, yes, after this healing you may find it easier to engage in life vigorously, using free will to follow today's new vibrational rules. Automatically your personal growth will accelerate.

4. End the vicious cycle of ET involvement

It can become a vicious cycle: the presence of more ETs can lead to a increased fascination with electronic substitutes for human reality, like video games or chat rooms or hours squandered texting about... not much.

- From an ET's perspective? When ETs look out through your human eyes, fantasy elements are pretty indistinguishable from what is humanly real. Colorful, trippy, amped-up reality pleases them. Therefore, the more time you spend on electronic amusements, the more attractive you become to ETs.

- From a human perspective? More spaciness results from increased ET influence. This, in turn, whets the appetite for more-more-more input that is not at a physical human level, such as involvement in a flashy fictional reality, addiction to video games, etc.

Fear not. With this healing complete, the vicious cycle of ET involvement case can slow down and, even, end. It can feel so good living with awareness positioned squarely at normal human vibrational frequencies!

A Teaching Tale of Energy Healing

While helping clients before the Shift, sometimes I would use the skill set that I have just taught you. Afterwards I would include research into how many ETs had been relocated. Usually that number would be in the hundreds; more rarely, a few thousand (especially for clients recovering from substance abuse).

Since the Shift, the numbers have grown dramatically. In 2015 I facilitated an ET Healing for my client Leo. Turned out, he unburdened himself of 49,000 ET entities.

Yes, you read that right. And yes, I used exactly the same skill set that you have just learned; afterwards just adding some research into how many ETs happened to leave.

Why are there so many more ETs now, impacting people like Leo? In this new Age of Awakening, flow is easier than ever before between human, astral, and Divine; so it may be easier than ever for ETs to visit. And with humans like us evolving way faster, I'm guessing that makes for a pretty spectacular light show.

- Appealing to first-time space tourists who never visited earth before.

- Fascinating, for comparison purposes, to those who visited back in the Age of Faith.

- Plus we have the arrival of opportunistic ETs: ambitious and eager to influence people who live in spiritual addiction; people who can come to welcome extreme spiritual addiction.

Whatever! Powerfully Human Reader, I'm so glad to help support your choice to live The New Strong. Use this latest skill set to help keep your aura healthy. Once more, you can depend on self-healing skills that activate your sacred Power of Command.

ET HEALING: QUICK VERSION — Okay, Quickish

Remember, Powerfully Human Reader, always do all three parts. Otherwise don't bother.

Speak this entire healing aloud. Substitute, if you wish, the name of a different ascended master or archangel for Archangel Gabriel.

1. Educate and release the ET entities

Archangel Gabriel, I call upon you to be here with me now in your Universal Cosmic Divine body of light. I awaken my Power of Command to co-create with you now. Place golden light around my aura and the place where I am now, so that only energies that are 100% helpful for my human life may enter at any time.

All you extraterrestrial beings, Dear Ones, I am speaking to each of you personally, along with Archangel Gabriel.

This is a healing ceremony just for you. Soon you will be relocated to your next, perfect place of expression.

Relax and receive this healing. You are safe. You are going to feel so much better soon. [Repeat for 30 seconds.]

Here are three gifts for you. Take at least a little bit of each one.

Gift #1 is Universal Cosmic Divine LOVE.

Gift #2 is Universal Cosmic Divine TRUTH.

Gift #3 is Universal Cosmic Divine LIGHT.

You are free from fear and pain and earth's vibrations, in this dimension and all other dimensions. Now Archangel Gabriel is going to escort you personally to your next place of development, the place that is right for you. Go in peace.

2. PUT IN appropriate energies

I call on Archangel Gabriel to fill this place and me with Universal Cosmic Divine Love, Universal Cosmic Divine Truth, and Universal Cosmic Divine Light.

I close off my aura so that only energies that are 100% helpful for my human life may enter at any time.

3. Complete the healing

Archangel Gabriel, find every astral tie between me and every ET entity involved with this healing, plus everyone I know in this world.

Please cut and dissolve all these astral ties, in every dimension. Then fill us with new love and light and peace.

Thank you, Archangel Gabriel. It is done. It is done. It is done.

Powerfully Human Reader, open your eyes. Success!

CHAPTER 21

New!
Remote Negative Thought Forms

Powerfully Human Reader, long before you found this Program for Easy Vibrational Balance, you were familiar with criticism. Sometimes it could happen behind your back. Far from the room where you are now, people can gossip about you, expressing jealousy or anger or other negative emotions.

Well, so what? It's bad karma for the one who complains. And serious gossip might cause you a bit of social inconvenience; otherwise does that impact you energetically in any significant way?

Used to be, the answer was "No." Unfortunately that answer has changed, given how energy moves in this Age of Awakening. Which is why I'm going to teach you how to fix the new problem of remote negative thought forms

Let's start with some practical education about what has changed.

Energetically What Used to Happen with Gossip

Used to be, you wouldn't be impacted energetically by somebody else's badmouthing. Not unless the two of you were either together in a room or talking on the phone, in which case there would be an astral-level impact.

Before we get to what's new, you may find it useful to learn about a kind of STUFF that has always been part of the earth experience. (And it has impacted you regardless of whether anyone told you about it in so many words.)

Let's start with an example. Consider that you're in the room with Wendell, a not-so-great friend who's a bit of a rageaholic. Suppose that he's busy gossiping to you about mutual friends.

Well, since you're talking directly with Wendell, every one of his nasty criticisms will result in equally nasty astral energies that stick to your aura, your clothes and surroundings.

What is the technical term for these astral bits of annoyance? NEGATIVE THOUGHT FORMS.

Book One in this series on Energy HEALING Skills has already given you a super-practical skill set for healing that kind of STUFF. Personally I love that Negative Thought Form Healing.

It doesn't just clean you up but provides the vibrational equivalent of new everything: an improved aura, better plumbing in your apartment, your favorite blue jeans vibrationally de-grimed. Yes, everything you own made energetically new!

So that self-healing skill in Book One can teach you how to clean up this annoying kind of STUFF. Negative thought forms have always been plentiful here at Earth School, a problem long before The Shift. And that hasn't changed, but...

What's Different Now?

Since the veil has gone, oops! Humans still have to deal with negative thought forms, but there's more. A new variation has emerged: REMOTE NEGATIVE THOUGHT FORMS.

These are totally healable, and you're going to learn the self-healing skills in our very next chapter. So fear not, Powerfully Human Reader, as I proceed to explain. Really it's quite interesting.

These destructive, malicious thought forms are hurled from a distance. Powerfully Human Reader, have you ever heard of remote healing, done by beautiful energy workers? It happens a bit like that. Only this variation is not beautiful at all, quite the opposite.

If it's any consolation, remote negative thought forms are usually sent by accident. If not necessarily intended to hurt you, why do they matter? Because STUFF is STUFF. Once formed, these astral objects in a person's aura are real, so they bring real consequences.

So what happens if somebody like Wendell is sitting around at home -- not near you at all -- and he happens to grumble about you? With the veil gone, his awareness can drop down suddenly... into a deep astral frequency... and send off the emotional equivalent of a fart. There she blows, a remote negative thought form that travels over to the inside your aura, where it sticks like glue.

Could be, he just mutters something quick, like "I can't stand that Susie." Fast as sending an email, that remote negative thought form lands in your inbox, as it were.

Such are the energetic times in which we live. Although you're not physically in the room with Wendell, STUFF happens. Thus, Wendell's grousing, grumpy "Phooey on you-ey" moment produces an astral-level object. Wow, materializing astral-level objects — and without having studied at Hogwarts!

Prior to learning the self-healing skill set for remote negative thought forms, what else is important to know about them? They vary enormously. Each of the 15 *kinds of STUFF* differs from the other 14 kinds. Then, *within its category*, a specific example of that kind of STUFF can also be unique.

For instance, one remote negative thought form might broadcast Wendell's jealousy. While another gives form to Wendell's momentary desire to poison your love life.

Fortunately, you won't have to probe into the sender or specific bouquet of ickiness belonging to each remote negative thought form. It's enough to just understand the basics.

    ~ What if Wendell sneers at you while visiting, sitting on your living room couch? You'll get a *regular* negative thought form. Extra versions will go into your clothes, your sofa, the wallpaper.

~ But if Wendell sends you that same sneer while not in your physical presence, now you'll receive a *remote* negative thought form. At least your sofa will be spared. Unlike regular negative thought forms, the remote ones will not lodge in physical objects. Only your aura is susceptible.

Great, in a way. Your sofa is fine. But how about you? At this very moment *you* could have plenty of astral-level daggers aurically stuck in your heart, your butt, any part of your body.

Well, how useful that you're learning this new skill set! One caution, though, Powerfully Human Reader. Please do not think of this problem as some deliberate kind of **PSYCHIC ATTACK**, where a person is out to get you energetically and succeeds at messing up your pristine aura.

Spare yourself. That kind of labelling might cause you to fear everybody who breathes out carbon dioxide. Such a scary way to live!

Black magic it ain't. Nevertheless, these astral-level objects can still be a real nuisance. So bring on an easy-peasy skill set to heal them right up.

CHAPTER 22

Another Useful Kind of Energy Cleanup

No need to wait passively while some frenemy like Wendell slings remote negative thought forms at you. Why live like a human dartboard? You're going to learn how to heal this STUFF right now.

Healing Remote Negative Thought Forms: PREPARE TO LEARN

Quaking in your shoes over the prospect of danger, hurled remotely? Nah, just keep your wits about you and calmly facilitate the healing.

Never, and I mean never, sit around hunting for STUFF caught in your energy field. What a waste of time, snooping around for remote negative thought forms! No brooding over lumps or bumps or tears in your auric field, either. At least not with RES.

Examining your energy field minutely may work for certain techniques of energy medicine that you have been taught. In which case, either do what you were taught or don't do the technique at all. Definitely keep that approach totally separate from anything connected with RES. You know better than to mix one healing modality with another, right?

It would be totally inappropriate to explore your energies for STUFF like remote negative thought forms, then try to figure out what it is shaped like or whom it came from. **ENERGY HYPO-CHONDRIA** is my name for that foolishness. *Regular hypochondria* involves brooding over illness that might exist in your physical body... except that it doesn't. *Energy hypochondria* involves brooding over illness that might exist in your energy field, as if brooding would fix a thing. In this Age of Awakening, how hard do you think it is to notice minute perturbations in your Force? (Minute and insignificant.)

Hey, you have a far more productive choice. Pay attention to human problems by noticing the who, what, where, and when. Then use common sense to solve that problem as best you can, either alone or with appropriate help. What if you have done that and still suspect that an *energetic* problem remains? Then choose one of our skill sets and use it.

More complex energy problems won't be resolved in that way, but at least you will have ruled out problems that can be addressed with self-healing; so, by all means, do that bit of self-healing. Afterwards you'll know if it's cost-effective to consult an RES expert.

How surprising is this? In the Age of Awakening, energy hypochondria is becoming much more common than before, especially in cases of spiritual addiction. To save yourself grief, trust human life. Besides that, when it comes to some quick self-healing that can help you feel better, trust the skill set that follows.

Healing Remote Negative Thought Forms: TEACHING VERSION

This particular skill set has four parts, required for you to receive the full benefit. Yes, it's our longest bunch o' steps in this Program for Easy Vibrational Balance. Are you surprised that I put it last? The skill set is easy; there's just a bit to it. Powerfully Human Reader, you can definitely do this.

PART ONE, REMOTE THOUGHT FORM HEALING.
Removal and put-in

Close your eyes. Notice how it feels to be you right now. How do you feel physically, emotionally, and/or mentally? Put words to the experience. Open your eyes and write something down, fast and sloppy —scribble-writing. Your Before Picture!

Say out loud, God, I call on you to be here with me now as a supercharged presence. I awaken my power of command to co-create with you now.

Please shine your light of truth into my physical and subtle bodies in every dimension. Identify every remote negative thought form that has lodged within me. Separate it out now.

Then lift the vibrations of each remote negative thought form until it dissolves into pure light and is completely recycled.

Immediately fill me with golden healing energy of Divine safety and blessing.

PART TWO, REMOTE THOUGHT FORM HEALING.
Imprint removal

Say out loud, God, when each remote negative thought form lodged within me, I also received vibrational imprints. So shine your light of truth into me again. Find and remove every vibrational imprint that has resulted from remote negative thought forms.

Recycle that energy. Then fill me up with more golden healing energy, awakening a fuller expression of my soul.

If any knowledge or experience is required for this healing to be both complete and permanent, please send it to me within three days, while I am sleeping or dreaming or first waking up in my day. Do this in a manner that is completely non-disruptive for these processes, plus falling asleep easily whenever I go to sleep. Thank you, God.

PART THREE, REMOTE THOUGHT FORM HEALING.
Adding forgiveness

Say out loud, Now that I have received this complete healing, help me to take the personal growth further. Awaken forgiveness *within me, a complete forgiveness of my past and also forgiveness of everyone who has sent remote negative thought forms my way.*

I have done the best I can in life. They have also done their best. I go free and I am willing to let them go free. From now on, a strong, glowing sense of identity protects me from anyone who wishes me harm.

PART FOUR, REMOTE THOUGHT FORM HEALING.
Start my new beginning

Say out loud, *God, please locate all astral ties between myself and everyone I know in the world, plus all sources of remote negative thought forms. Cut and dissolve all those astral ties and then make available new love, light, and peace. Thank you, God. It is done. It is done. It is done.*

Close your eyes. Notice how it feels to be you right now. How do you feel physically, emotionally, and/or mentally? Put words to the experience. Write this down, fast and sloppy — scribble-writing. That's your After Picture.

Open your eyes. Look over your Before-and-After Picture. What changed for you? Even a subtle shift would count as an immediate result.

Healing Remote Negative Thought Forms: RESULTS

How does it feel to be you right now? With every part of this skill set, removal of astral STUFF has been followed by PUT IN for a stronger *soul* expression.

By now you know better than ever the meaning of that word SOUL. No mere abstract concept, your soul matters. So very human, your soul is like a dog wagging his tail. Expressing your soul means that you are joyfully being yourself (and not trying to be anything else).

STUFF moved out, then you PUT IN what helps you to live fully juicy, being yourself. That's soul expression, folks.

Healing Remote Negative Thought Forms: HOW THIS TECHNIQUE HELPS YOU

Astral-level garbage can limit us in so many ways. Remote negative thought forms are a perfect example. Maybe you have heard the saying, "That which does not kill me makes me stronger."

Eventually? Maybe. I agree that, *after* recovery from that which has threatened your life, you may be stronger. But let's be sensible, Powerfully Human Reader. Carrying poison around in your system, such as a remote negative thought form? Not something to make you stronger, not for the weeks, months, or years that you tote it around.

Here are examples of remote negative thought forms: Ambivalence, confusion, absent-mindedness, even self-loathing. Well, buh-bye. And good riddance!

Healing Remote Negative Thought Forms: QUICK VERSION

1. Healing the Remote Negative Thought Forms

God, I call on you to be here with me now as a supercharged presence. I awaken my power of command to co-create with you now.

Please shine your light of truth into my physical and subtle bodies in every dimension. Identify every remote negative thought form that has lodged within me. Separate it out now.

Then lift the vibrations of each remote negative thought form until it dissolves into pure light and is completely recycled.

Immediately fill me with golden healing energy of Divine safety and blessing.

2. Imprint Removal

God, when each remote negative thought form lodged within me, I also received vibrational imprints. So shine your light of truth into me again. Find and remove every vibrational imprint that has resulted from remote negative thought forms.

Recycle that energy. Then fill me up with more golden healing energy, awakening a fuller expression of my soul.

If any knowledge or experience is required for this healing to be both complete and permanent, please send it to me within three days, while I am sleeping or dreaming or first waking up in my day. Do this in a manner that is completely non-disruptive for these processes, plus falling asleep easily whenever I go to sleep. Thank you, God.

3. Adding Forgiveness

Now that I have received this complete healing, help me to take the personal growth further. Awaken forgiveness within me, a complete forgiveness of my past and also forgiveness of everyone who has sent remote negative thought forms my way.

I have done the best I can in life. They have also done their best. I go free and I am willing to let them go free. From now on, a strong, glowing sense of identity protects me from anyone who wishes me harm.

4. Start My New Beginning

God, please locate all astral ties between myself and everyone I know in the world, plus all sources of remote negative thought forms.

Cut and dissolve all those astral ties and then make available new love, light, and peace. Thank you, God. It is done. It is done. It is done.

PART FIVE

More Ways to Strengthen Yourself Vibrationally

Would you like to live in the Age of Awakening? Well, it's too late to weigh in on that one.

But you can choose whether or not to take advantage of this non-negotiable, wonderfully historic opportunity. And you are. Powerfully Human Reader, you're becoming an EARLY ADAPTER.

That happens when a person begins to behave like an EARLY ADOPTER, a first person to learn something that is relatively new in the world. Using recommendations from our Program for Easy Vibrational Balance, by adopting, you will *adapt* extra fast and live exceptionally comfortably in the Age of Awakening.

Every gentle change you make can greatly accelerate your adjustment to living on earth with no veil left, and a tendency of awareness to slip-slide into the astral. That's a lot to adapt to, but...

If you continue to put human frequencies first, you will evolve super-quick. And without working hard to keep fixing yourself!

So far you've learned the 10 essential rules for thriving today, plus you're using several new tools in the form of skill sets.

Now let's help you adapt further. We'll add some other practical tools, as well as the more advanced concepts that accompany them. Part Five can help you grow even more comfortable with using your 20 Daily Minutes of Technique Time, Tops.

Working longer than that on self-growth is actually counterproductive, now that the veil is gone. Let's explore how to make the most of that super-productive resource for all of us living now, daily Technique Time.

Use that time productively and you can expect to find many annoying old problems in life simply lose their hold on you.

Meanwhile, you'll become more successful at human goals that you care about, like more love, filling your social calendar with quality relationships, making more money, helping others more effectively.

Human happiness *your* way — bring it on!

CHAPTER 23

Your Personal
List of Techniques

Powerfully Human Reader, thanks to Part Four, you're cleaned up energetically. So your thinking is clearer than ever. Yet you still may find it confusing: what really counts as Technique Time and what doesn't?

Until that's clear, how can you possibly get with the program? So this chapter aims to refine your understanding about options for personal growth. They're various and they're wonderful.

At least some are wonderful.

Personally, I wouldn't do certain forms of Technique Time if you paid me! What does it matter if a technique is famous or popular? That doesn't mean it will necessarily help *you*. Many techniques from the Age of Faith don't work well now, and that's especially true of many practices from the New Age years.

Complicating matters, the sheer number of techniques is overwhelming. In this chapter I'll list 100, and this list is far from complete.

Still, you may recognize some things you've done and also the process of reading may cause you think of *other* techniques — not listed here — that you've been doing.

Well, might I suggest this? As you proceed down my not-quite-complete-list, make your own version. This will become your personal list for ACCELERATING MY PERSONAL GROWTH.

After you finish this chapter, keep that list around and add to it as new ideas occur to you, both *new ideas* for techniques you might do, plus techniques you've been *choosing* to do, and also — oops! — little things you've been doing that still count as Technique Time, even if *you never realized it before.*

To help you follow through on this Program for Easy Vibrational Balance, keep that list current and consult it as needed.

Maybe you'll also remember to be kind to yourself along the way. Fact is, you weren't raised to keep track of Technique Time; that wasn't needed back in the day. You weren't raised in the Age of Awakening, were you?

Get yourself up to speed gently, okay? No excuses. And no being mean to yourself, either! The concept is clear and clean, once you get it: Either an activity counts as Technique Time or it doesn't.

Besides treating yourself nicely, what else can help as you create that list for Accelerating My Personal Growth?

- Reading the examples here, you may find it simple to recognize when you've been doing forms of **OFFICIAL TECHNIQUE TIME.** These self-growth practices have official names, definitions, do's and don'ts, etc. Just don't expect my names to be identical with yours. It's a *type* of inner activity.

- Please take a little extra time when you read through examples of **UNOFFICIAL TECHNIQUE TIME.** Because you might need more thought to recognize whether you've been doing them. You see, these personal practices don't necessarily have any name at all that you would recognize. Hey, they're unofficial!

Clients like Jack have told me, "I never set out to do this on purpose. I guess I just fell into it." That is common for an ambitious, self-actualizing person... who just happens to be living in this new Age of Awakening... and hasn't learned yet how to adapt.

Understandably, we can wind up doing unofficial self-improvement for two hours a day, five hours, or longer; with most of it done in little bits and pieces, off and on.

This techniquing isn't consciously recognized as such, let alone counted. Until, maybe, now.

So here's what I'll list for you: separate examples of official and unofficial practices. Also I'll categorize growth practices as either *spiritual* or *psychological* -- although, with any of these techniques, you may be aiming for both kinds of improvement.

Remember, Powerfully Human Reader, you can choose to do any combo you like: official or unofficial, spiritual or psychological. Just limit each day's total Technique Time to 20 minutes, maximum.

25 OFFICIAL Forms of
Spiritually-Oriented Technique Time

1. Prayer, with awareness removed from everyday life and your heart lifted up towards God.

2. Meditation with eyes closed, using a method that you have learned.

3. Contemplation, whether religious or mystical or spiritual or New Agey.

4. Mystical forms of movement like Praise Dancing, Sufi Dancing.

5. Creative visualization; picturing or imagining what you desire.

6. Spiritual exercise, whether guided by others or done in a group.

7. Any other kind of spiritual exercise that is done for self-growth, including experiments with the paranormal that you do out of curiosity.

8. Breathing exercises to elevate your consciousness.

9. Meditation done with eyes open, such as walking a labyrinth or doing a mindfulness meditation.

10. Working with a prayer partner or other spiritual counsellor.

11. Seeking upliftment through *reading* scripture or uplifting books or websites… about the sacred or celestial or miraculous.

12. *Watching* videos or *listening* to podcasts or *talking* to friends on the topics just mentioned.

13. Bible study.

14. Going to a religious service where you get "in the spirit," do faith healing, or practice the laying on of hands.

15. Psychic development exercises.

16. Channeling astral beings.

17. Mediumship.

18. Readings with tarot cards or other forms of divination that require intuition. (Opening a fortune cookie doesn't count.)

19. Yoga, where you do an asana and then notice the impact with eyes closed before going on to the next posture. (This contrasts with "Gym yoga," which uses traditional asanas as a kind of exercise, done without noticing the inner impact of each posture.)

20. Other energy-based movement for spiritual development, like Tai Chi or Qi Gong.

21. Energy healing to cleanse your aura, balance your chakras, etc.

22. Energy healing for emotions, like Emotional Freedom Technique or saying affirmations.

23. Energy healing for your physical health, like Reiki or using crystals.

24. Doing freestyle energy readings to better understand yourself or others, including tools that might inspire you like angel cards.

25. Doing aura reading or Skilled Empath Merge with skills taught to you by a teacher.

25 UNOFFICIAL Forms of
Spiritually-Oriented Technique Time

1. Improvised prayers during your day.

2. Asking God or saints for guidance, as needed.

3. Pausing to ask yourself, "What would God have me do?" or "What would Jesus do?"

4. A kind of spiritual multi-tasking, where you're not just going through your daily activities but, simultaneously, conducting a detached search for meaning. For instance, while having a fight with your co-worker, you're silently pondering: "Everything happens for a reason. What is this conversation supposed to be teaching me?"

5. Depth self-awareness during exercise, like lifting weights in a way where you aim to feel every minute impact of every move you make.

6. "Also contemplating the meaning of life," for instance, while walking down the street or reading your emails.

7. Seeking synchronicity (and maybe also aiming to attract miracles).

8. Peppering ordinary life with affirmations or inspirational slogans.

9. During everyday activity, secretly detaching so you can examine in detail your physical sensations (and not because you're in pain but because this has become an interesting hobby).

10. Trying to live from your heart or Higher Self or spirit.

11. Striving to act "deeply authentic" or "spiritually whole."

12. In order to recharge, detaching from the situation you're in and going to your "happy place."

13. Closing your eyes for a few moments so that you can feel peace, remember spirit, etc.

14. Frequently stopping whatever you're doing so that you can ground and shield your energies, a.k.a. "Be in your body."

15. Before you speak or act, checking to see if the energy feels right.

16. *Actively seeking* advice from your guides or *staying open* to psychic hits which could come at any moment.

17. Using muscle testing or a pendulum to make everyday choices.

18. Making decisions based mainly on intuition or energies.

19. In the course of your daily activity, volunteering to *bless* people, for example, by sending them good vibes.

20. In the course of your daily activities, volunteering to *heal* people energetically, such as "Sending them love and light."

21. Trying to improve relationships by reading people's energies.

22. Trying to solve conflicts by vibing out "What is really going on?"

23. Picking up people's vibes or seeing auras because "I can't help it." (Sure you can.)

24. Noticing energies because "That's what I do." (Doesn't have to be....

25. Multi-tasking during conversations by secretly checking out people's energies.

25 OFFICIAL Forms of Psychologically-Oriented Technique Time

1. Having a session with a mental health professional where you are invited to re-experience upsetting feelings at a deep level.

2. Having a session with a mental health professional where you are required to delve into your past.

3. Having a session with a mental health professional where you are coached to step outside your regular ways of thinking and change them.

4. Having a session with a mental health professional where you are guided to find and face your fears.

5. Having a session with a mental health professional that aims to revisit and resolve traumas from your past.

6. Having a session with a mental health professional that teaches you to detach from life, to find your patterns, or to analyze how you are stuck.

7. Doing any homework for personal growth assigned by a mental health professional.

8. Assigning *yourself* homework, as if you were your own therapist.

9. Taking time to figure out how to resolve your issues.

10. Taking time to identify your causes of negative thinking.

11. Taking time to understand your emotional triggers.

12. Taking time to replay a conversation and stay in touch with your feelings, as if you were meeting with a therapist.

13. Taking time to examine strong feelings that you have had during your day.

14. Taking time to figure out how you can rid yourself of negative thoughts and emotions.

15. Taking time to express your deep feelings and explore how they are related to your emotional patterns.

16. Using self-help books (or other resources) to analyze your patterns.

17. Using self-help books (or other resources) to learn who you really are.

18. Using self-help books (or other resources) to heal your past.

19. Using self-help books (or other resources) to change how you speak to people.

20. Using self-help books (or other resources) to think about people you know and figure out their problems.

21. Using self-help books (or other resources) to identify narcissists and protect yourself from them.

22. Using self-help books (or other resources) to identify people with codependency and protect yourself from them.

23. While with people, purposely analyzing your thoughts and thought patterns, seeking to understand the cause.

24. While with people, purposely examining your patterns so that you can understand why you do what you do.

25. While with people, purposely multi-tasking by working on your issues.

25 UNOFFICIAL Forms of Psychologically-Oriented Technique Time

1. In everyday life, habitually trying to be yourself.

2. In everyday life, habitually trying to see your patterns.

3. Habitually seeking new insights into your issues.

4. Habitually observing yourself, evaluating whether or not you're making progress psychologically.

5. Multi-tasking in everyday life by changing your spontaneous response to make it (supposedly) better.

6. Habitually trying to improve communication by applying psychological concepts you've learned.

7. Habitually trying to improve communication by analyzing what the other person is "really" trying to tell you.

8. Habitually trying to improve communication by sharing your deeper, "authentic" feelings about the situation.

9. Trying to improve communication by shifting the conversation to process. What are the underlying dynamics and patterns of this relationship? (Maybe discussing this out loud; maybe keeping track mentally in a detached manner.)

10. Multi-tasking in everyday life by applying *any* technique that you have learned for improving relationships.

11. Assessing your emotional state, off and on, in order to make psychological progress. Perhaps trying to decide, about that thing you just said, "Was it healthy?"

12. Trying to pinpoint the causes of your current emotions — yes, along with feeling them — more multi-tasking.

13. Catching when you feel negative and doing all you can to stay positive.

14. Catching when you feel negative and trying to heal yourself on the spot by understanding the hidden reasons why you feel that way.

15. Flagging times when you feel bad, then probing to figure out why you feel that way.

16. Flagging times when you're upset, and staying with that feeling until it passes.

17. Watching for when your issues flare up, then seeking to discover new hidden memories that were causes.

18. Evaluating your moods... and when they're not good, reassuring yourself, "And that's okay."

19. Trying to avoid negative people.

20. Trying to avoid narcissists.

21. Trying to avoid so-called "psychic vampires."

22. Trying to avoid being emotionally triggered.

23. Trying to calm down and relax.

24. In your spare time, reviewing and replaying past traumas or frustrations, etc.

25. During times of stress, not just spontaneously speaking and doing things but, instead, trying to do something that's more psychologically savvy. (Perhaps also pretending that you are with your therapist.)

VIBRATIONAL Perspective on Technique Time

Powerfully Human Reader, you've first-drafted that list for Accelerating My Personal Growth. Congratulations! Long or short, it's valuable. Let's enhance that value by applying a vibrational perspective.

Why does every single activity on your list count as Technique Time? Because Technique Time begins whenever you *actively pursue experiences* that are not at human frequencies.

That includes *multi-tasking with awareness*. Not human-level multi-tasking, like doing the laundry while you listen to music. **MULTI-TASKING WITH AWARENESS** happens when you're doing something vibrationally human like washing your clothes and, in addition, you jazz this up by positioning your awareness at something "deeper" or "more productive."

These are astral frequencies.

> What, even if the subject matter is Divine, like trying to practice the presence of God? Probably you're multi-tasking at an astral frequency. And so it counts as Technique Time.
> Note: If spontaneous experiences of the Divine come into your life, you might notice a peace or a glow... but not because you are doing anything. This is a kind of grace. It flows, like tea brewing gently in water. And your awareness is not divided but enhanced, clearer and tastier.

> How about psychological exploration of your human life? Say howdy to your subconscious! Vibrationally that's where your awareness will travel, despite physically going through the motions of doing the laundry.

> Also, it counts as Technique Time if you *let yourself drift* into a spaced-out state, not making contact with human reality.

Can you really do this while folding your laundry? Definitely.

When you're *going through the motions,* this Technique Time may not show to others. Nonetheless, your inner awareness is not positioned at human frequencies. So, whether you admit it or not, it's Technique Time.

I wonder, Powerfully Human Reader, have you met people like Felix? He describes himself as "Coming from a high vibrational place," as though this makes him superior.

Nonsense! "Higher vibrations" bring dazzle. Any pothead can "attain" them. But favoring astral experience is not a superior way for humans to live. Far from making extra progress at his personal growth, Felix is being sidetracked.

Make no mistake. Living at "higher vibrations" helps nobody to evolve, producing neither spiritual Enlightenment nor psychological self-actualization. By definition, human vibrations aren't astral or Divine. Our human frequencies are purposely designed to be lower than astral vibes, designed as appropriate for us earthlings.

With the veil gone, is it still appropriate to live human-based? Now, when energies are so much fun to explore? Yes, human experience matters still. Because, hey, we signed up for Earth School!

Fear not, Powerfully Human Reader. When you adapt well to human reality as it is today, those funky human experiences can turn absolutely glorious.

PRACTICAL Perspective on Technique Time

From a practical perspective, "Technique Time" simply means trying to grow as a person. In this chapter, I've been encouraging you to stop overdoing that. Too much fixing yourself, ironically, slows down personal growth.

Instead you can have personal development done on purpose! Done in the way you choose! Effective use of your time! While making a limited time commitment, because that dedicated time is so powerful!

During your chosen Technique Time, you won't position awareness at objective reality, what human beings say and do. Instead:

∿ You're trying to grow spiritually.

～ Or else there's a psychological emphasis.

～ Either way, taking a vacation from regular human-type thoughts and feelings, you strive for a deeper and more *meaningful* experience.

But what are you to do all day long, if not that?

Human-level thoughts and feelings are different from their astral versions. Again, think Matroyshka dolls; only the different subtleties of consciousness are not obviously different, like taking a large wooden doll and unscrewing her head and then popping out the smaller-sized doll.

Some of my students have found this subtle difference confusing.

Gladys asked me, "Astral? How can it be astral if I'm thinking and feeling about my *human* life?"

My answer: "The subject of your thoughts is different from the process. One process is to have regular down-to-earth thoughts and feelings. This process has a different quality from scrunching up your forehead, or holding your breath, or looking at the ceiling while you start moving your consciousness in an astral direction."

Gladys continued, "How can I be human without my thoughts and feelings?"

My answer: "That's the point. You already have plenty of human thoughts and feelings. Only many a sophisticated person considers them obvious, trivial, or boring.

"With psychological overwork or spiritual addiction, regular human-level experiences are habitually thrust aside in favor of something more special.

"It's like, 'Why just walk when I could balance on tiptoe, waving my arms and creating a beautiful dance?' Well, I'm asking you to get back to walking. Save the fancy-dancing for 20 minutes per day."

Finally, Gladys asked me, "What if I happen to think and feel deeply? How can I be *me* without that? Isn't the essence of my humanity that I don't think and feel as instinctive reactions?"

Yes, part of the beauty of Gladys' soul is that depth. But maybe she has been emphasizing that depth to such an extent that she has been ignoring the shallows — human-level vibrational frequencies. With ordinary thinking, a person can also reflect.

I told her, "We don't need to transcend everyday life in order to learn or develop compassion." Gladys got it. The difference is subtle. Yet she found her way to understand it, just as you can. And now she is growing faster than ever before.

Powerfully Human Reader, what can you look forward to once you drop the habit of fixing yourself? Every day can be so much fun. Imagine... you're fully engaged in the variety of each day at Earth School; saying things and doing things, learning as best you can from *everyday* experience. More than ever, you enjoy the fruits of your labors. Especially sweet, you become more effective at helping other people.

Guess what else? Another benefit is that you find yourself automatically following the 10 new vibrational rules. Receiving support of nature. Spontaneously you are living The New Strong.

You Have So Many Excellent Choices

Once you get the knack, there's great freedom in distinguishing regular human activities from Technique Time. Let's conclude this chapter with an example. At work, Project Manager Lucy is writing a progress report. Would the following activities count as Technique Time or not?

- Lucy tracks what her assistant Griffin has done lately. *No, Not Technique Time. Regular human-level activity.*

- Griffin hasn't completed a project she gave him. Project Manager Lucy tries to figure out how to solve this problem.

> What can she do or say? *No, Not Technique Time. Regular human-level activity.*

- ∾ Lucy worries about what's going on with Griffin on a deeper level, causing his behavior. She tries to understand at depth how he feels. *Yes, Technique Time.*

- ∾ Lucy wonders if she has attracted this behavior from Griffin because of some bad energies she's been carrying. *Yes, Technique Time.*

- ∾ After work, Lucy sits down for personal growth time. She uses 10 of that day's 20 minutes to analyze her situation with Griffin from a psychological perspective. *Yes, Technique Time,* and this is an Official Version of Technique Time rather than the two other Unofficial Versions of Technique Time listed previously.

Like Lucy, some of your choices are better than others. Once you put your mind to it, you can figure out what's what.

Don't squander this precious lifetime on a mishmash of unofficial Technique Time self-help. Decide how you will spend those precious 20 minutes, and then follow through.

Powerfully Human Reader, are you a little surprised that you might have needed some coaching on something like this? One way or another, all people who live on earth now... have been struggling to adapt. Our new vibrational freedom is unprecedented. Adjusting to life without the veil? This has been tough for us all.

In ways that are entirely new for human beings, we have dominion over where we position our consciousness. That is a very big deal. Please have patience with yourself as you get used to this very new way of using your free will: 20 Daily Minutes of Technique Time. Count the rest as brain fog.

Meanwhile, it can be such a habit, drifting around in awareness. Okay, you've been coached to handle such space-out times as though they are brain fog. But how, exactly, can you make yourself stop? Our next chapter will explain exactly what to do.

CHAPTER 24

Reinsert Yourself into Reality

Dylan got with the program, this Program for Easy Vibrational Balance — which is good, since psychological overwork had become a very big problem for him. Dylan has cut way down on Technique Time. Now he does just 20 minutes at lunch hour.

But Dylan has a guilty secret. He daydreams. A lot. "Can't help it," Dylan told me. Then he asked, "If it keeps on happening, will that matter?"

Indeed! Prolonged daydreaming can sabotage your effectiveness in life.

Until he learned how to stop this pattern, Dylan didn't know what to do about all that daydreaming. But once he found out, this became a non-problem for him. What you'll read about in this chapter just might help you, too.

"Daydreaming" Is Only One of Many Names

Alternatively you could call this problem DAYDREAMING or BRAIN FOG or AWAY MOMENTS or SPACING OUT or GOING TO MY HAPPY PLACE or plenty of other names. For simplicity, I'll stick to the term "brain fog."

Brain fog means random moments of not making contact with objective reality even though you're awake, with eyes open. Sometimes there are physical causes that can be remedied relatively easily, including problems with diet, not getting enough sleep, or smoking pot. Sometimes help from a mental health professional is needed.

Yet none of this explains why *so many people* today suffer from brain fog. In my opinion, many instances are caused by slow adaptation to Earth School's altered vibrational reality, including the 10 new vibrational rules in this Age of Awakening.

One of my students, an attorney, noted that brain fog, "really seems to be part of the soup we are all swimming in right now."

By now, Powerfully Human Reader, you know what kind of soup that is: living in the Age of Awakening, with no more veil. Brain fog happens to just about everyone now, and far more frequently than 10 or 20 years ago.

The question is what to do about it. This Program for Easy Vibrational Balance includes three more tools for helping you to adapt. Coming right up in this chapter.

Tool #1 for Brain Fog: Understanding

Understand what? Know when what's happening to you does NOT count as brain fog.

Given that you're a human adult, regarding the flow of awareness, it's natural that for certain times of day… your awareness will not be terribly focused.

Within your first half hour (or so) of waking up each day

Early each day, your consciousness may scamper all over the place. For instance:

- Images or feelings from your dreams.
- Random thoughts about yesterday.
- Making plans for today.
- Thoughts about God.
- Thoughts about sex.
- A yearning for coffee.

Well none of that counts, at least in terms of brain fog. Going through your usual waking-up ritual will be plenty to get you functioning in your new day's reality.

Certain activities are part of a normal human lifestyle

Awareness can get flowy under circumstances like these:

- Before or after making love, or while planning for that hot date. (But for a number of minutes, not hours, right? Even Viagra manufacturers say four hours straight is too long.)
- While engaged in any creative activity, like photography or singing.
- While exercising, such as jogging, tennis, or playing golf.
- After a beer or a glass of wine.

By now you understand about Technique Time. That's different, right?

Jogging, for instance, can get you into a state of flow. That's not brain fog. Just don't "improve it" by communing with spirit guides.

Or say that you're hanging with friends, having a beer, talking together. And maybe you're slightly sloshed. That's ok, so long as you're not also trying to imagine that you're really in a cafe carousing with a bunch of space aliens from the original "Star Wars" movie.

Just be the human person, paying a reasonable amount of attention to other people and your surroundings. Of course, it's up to you, adjusting your everyday lifestyle so that you're in a productive balance for you.

Five hours a day drinking beer? Sadly, that lifestyle imbalance would contribute to a different kind of brain fog. Accordingly, that topic would warrant a different sort of conversation.

This chapter isn't about problems with alcohol but, rather, how to avoid the NO-VEIL BRAIN FOG that happens to just about everyone in this Age of Awakening. When people aren't drinking booze or smoking weed.

After you go to bed for the night

Regardless of your schedule, there will be a time that you identify as "Bedtime." That's what I'm referring to here.

Once you land in that bed, in terms of your awareness, anything goes. If you fall asleep right away, congratulations. But if it takes a while for you to drift into slumber, do whatever you like with awareness.

- Pray or meditate.
- Contemplate your navel.
- Visualize your chakras in pleasing colors.
- Reflect on the day's social interactions and analyze away.

None of this counts as Technique Time, either. Once you hit that futon (or whatever), it counts as pre-sleep. Your awareness may be moving in and out of sleep or dreaming or whatever. So have fun!

There's the bright side of insomnia, right?

Tool #2 for Brain Fog: Recognize and Use Your Moment of Choice

Suppose that you're driving your car or sitting at your usual place at work. Suddenly it dawns on you:

Hello! I've drifted away. I'm in brain fog.

Recognize this **MOMENT OF CHOICE**. When the brain fog began, you got no official notification, no screech like a smoke alarm.

- Instead you drifted away from doing a human-type job.
- Awareness slipped into a different positioning of consciousness, an astral-level experience.

Understand this, Powerfully Human Reader. Different vibrational frequencies are not labeled in life. Yes, brain fog means having awareness positioned at an astral version of life, not at human vibrational frequencies.

The *content* seems human, but the *process* of paying attention is astral.

Does that seem very abstract? Here come some concrete examples.

- You might be replaying some past incident with Pat when the two of you were in Paris.
- Or you're noticing Pat's sweet energies.
- Or you're analyzing your issues as a couple.
- Or you're daydreaming about the future.
- Or you have no clear idea exactly where you have been drifting, but then you realize...
- Hello! You've been somewhere, not here.

In vibrational terms, what do all these space-outs have in common? Your awareness has shifted from human vibrational frequencies over to the astral.

Ergg! No way was that a choice. But once you realize what has been going on, *now* you have a choice. It could go either way:

- Continue to daydream about Pat or Paris or whatever? OR
- Hello! Switch back to the here and now. Get back to work, fold that laundry, whatever.

If you choose to daydream, that's Technique Time. Taking this extra time counts. Such moments can easily take you way past the 20 minutes, maximum, for a balanced life.

By contrast, how about that initial away moment? That didn't count as Technique Time because no choice was involved.

Okay, say that you're convinced now. You'd like to make the choice away from that unofficial Technique Time. How, exactly, do you return to here and now, human-style? The answer can be very simple.

Whenever you have a choice about where to position your consciousness, re-engage in whatever you were doing right before the brain fog. Maybe spice it up just a bit.

That sums up your first tool for un-fogging the brain. Very often, it's ridiculously simple to re-engage in whatever activity you were doing right before the brain fog.

Just find a way to make that activity more interesting now. Take a different approach to that assignment at work. Or turn your laundry folding into a challenging race, trying to get it done super-quick.

Whatever you're doing, make it fun.

Or else take a little break to goof off in human ways, like stretching.

Usually it is way simple to re-engage in whatever you were doing. And then, automatically, your awareness will make a gentle vibrational shift back to human frequencies.

Tool #3 for Brain Fog:
Reinsert Yourself into Reality

What if, despite the second tool proposed here, you still have trouble getting back to that project at work or that not-so-thrilling heap of laundry?

Conveniently you happen to be human, and living on earth. Did you know? Human-level objective reality can help so much for the appropriate positioning of your consciousness.

Physical things that you can touch or watch, hear or smell: these exist at human vibrational frequencies, right? So they can help you to snap out of brain fog.

Because you have both a human nervous system and (believe it or not) sanity, you can use physical reality to move awareness back from the astral. Just reinsert yourself into physical reality:

- Physically get up and walk around.
- Pick up an object and move it, like drawing with a pencil.
- Stretch. (If you are with other people, your more discreet version is fidgeting. That can work.)
- Touch a few different textures.
- Talk to someone. Or whistle. Or yodel.
- Find something good to smell and take a sniff.
- Jump up and down until you get winded.

Within a minute, your awareness will be back, positioned in human vibrational frequencies. Then go back to whatever you were doing before the brain fog. (And maybe spice it up a little.)

Warning: What Won't Help You One Bit

Powerfully Human Reader, the tools you've been given will work. If you use them. Just don't try to substitute self-talk or personal introspection. Choices like the following will actually take you deeper into brain fog:

- Trying to adjust your thoughts or feelings so that you can "be more in the present."
- Blaming yourself for drifting off. (Hey, it happens to everyone. And blaming can lead to additional astral-type disconnect from regular human-level experience.)
- Attempting to "ground" your energies.
- Interpreting how the brain fog makes you feel.
- Analyzing the brain fog as if this has become your latest psychological "issue."
- Doing any other kind of Technique Time activity (like prayer, asking for guidance, auto-suggestion) in order to

stop the brain fog.

Just keep things simple, Smarty. Reinsert yourself into physical reality and consider the problem solved. It will be.

Note: Tools are great but they don't fix everything. A screwdriver won't do the job of a drill.

So it's possible that, when trying to use the three tools in this chapter, you've still got a problem with brain fog. What to do then?

- If you're still functioning pretty well in everyday life, consider a session of aura healing with RES. Because other energetic factors could be involved, astral-level forms of STUFF that can still be healed but require professional skills for STUFF removal.

- But what if you're struggling, and maybe even not functioning that well right now? Seek help from a mental health professional.

Getting this kind of help doesn't mean "You're crazy." It just means, "You're getting help from a person who knows how to solve the kind of problem you're having."

One way or another, you can definitely vanquish brain fog. For The New Strong, it's important to find a way to inhabit your human life, here and now.

You're on the right planet, Powerfully Human Reader. Earth School is not A Candyland of Space-Out.

Still, life on earth can become appropriately sweet with this chapter's easy-to-use tools. You've learned a lot in this chapter about how to position consciousness appropriately. Good old Earth School, a fine place to live!

CHAPTER 25

Seven Success Stories

Powerfully Human Reader, I love your insistence on persistence. Hasn't it begun to pay off? One chapter at a time, you have learned so much. And in our next chapter you will graduate from this Program for Easy Vibrational Balance.

In advance I would like to give you this chapter as a graduation present.

You see, on a regular basis I am inspired by success stories from RES clients, practitioners, and apprentices. Here I will share seven of my favorites. Each one concerns adjusting to the new vibrational rules in this Age of Awakening.

Incidentally, if you wind up having a success story to send me, don't be shy.

- Send an email to stories@rose-rosetree.com.
- Or mail me a letter c/o Women's Intuition Worldwide, 116 Hillsdale Dr., Sterling, VA 20164

Now, use your eyes to unwrap these seven presents. May they manage to warm your post-postmodern heart!

Each of these teaching tales was written by a (now) Powerfully Human Reader.

1. A Psychiatrist's Just-in-Time Wakeup Call

As a psychiatrist (and a grateful recipient of many sessions of Rosetree Energy Spirituality) I am well aware that spiritual addiction, like any addiction, can worsen any mental imbalance and can also lead to mental health emergencies.

This is my story of spiritual addiction, which also coincided with my introduction to RES.

Perhaps, like many people, when I first became interested in spirituality I was naive. I sampled many, many spiritual teachings without understanding the need to carefully consider the integrity of the teacher or the message.

I was well-balanced mentally, and certainly I never considered the wisdom of limiting my exposure to spiritual teachings or, in the parlance of RES, "Limiting my Technique Time."

I recall feeling something along the lines of "the more, the better." I was excited about my spiritual discoveries.

Later I realized that my unexamined assumption that the spirit world, just by virtue of not being in human form, contained wisdom unavailable to me... led me to over-consume spiritual teachings without discretion, to my detriment.

I began feeling an odd disconnection to my human life. It wasn't unpleasant really, and I enjoyed the relief from all kinds of human discomfort and pain.

Gradually I began noticing that I couldn't get any traction in my work or my relationships.

It felt as if *any effective action in the human world that might occur to me to solve a problem... was just outside my reach*, and I almost didn't care anyway.

I can't recall exactly, but that may have been why I arranged a session with Rose.

In our very first session Rose gently introduced me to the concept of spiritual addiction, although she may not have used that specific term at the time, and she also used the Vibrational Re-Positioning® healing technique.

Now I'm back, solidly and effectively engaging in my human life.

Following this and other sessions with Rose, I became a much more informed consumer of spiritual teachings.

Although my experience with spiritual addiction was relatively brief and did not lead to a mental health emergency, without Rose's help and the teachings of RES I'm not sure where my disengagement with my human life would have led me.

— Arthur Rosenberg, M.D., Madison, Wisconsin

2. When Spiritual Addiction Leads to a Breakdown

I was introduced to New Age Spirituality in early 2010 after going to a hypnotist to quit smoking.

I'd started cigarettes again, after successfully giving them up years before. This time around, smoking helped me to cope with a traumatic experience that shook my world.

Desperate to stop smoking now, I had three hypnosis sessions. They didn't work. I felt worse.

After the last session I was so bad with vomiting, a pounding head and slurred speech… my hubby took me to hospital, where they thought I'd had a stroke or brain bleed. It was a migraine, a shockingly bad one.

Still Desperate for Help

The lovely hypnotist, who had become a friend, then introduced me to angels, meditation, and Doreen Virtue.

I attended one of her Empowerment Workshops and did a meditation. I began weeping uncontrollably as red appeared during this process. This reminded me of my abusive father.

In this group meditation I felt that I received an important message, which was "Forgiveness is the key." I began to search for a way to forgive my father, let go of the hatred and anger I had towards him, and be a better person all around.

Spending More and More Time on Self-Improvement

I soaked up all I could.

The Law of Attraction was new to me; I bought books and CD's.

I had healings with one very reputable energy healer.

Then I started just to want to learn more. So, over the course of a year, this is what I did:

- Graduated from Reiki Levels 1, 2, and 3
- Explored crystal healing
- Took a shamanic healing course
- Bought oracle cards and more books
- Purchased smudge sticks
- Began to use a ceremonial drum.

My desire to connect to the Divine was strong. Then an incident with one healer set me back. He told me that within me he found evil, ghosts, and a curse.

For nine months I had anxiety. One day I vowed no more spiritual stuff... but the very next day my psychic development teacher contacted me. She was running a Reiki Master's Class. So away I went.

My Interpretation? Synchronicity.

Divine timing! Obviously the Divine didn't want me to give up my spiritual practice!

I still slept with the light on when hubby was away. Socially I shut myself off. By then, I'd left my well-paying job because of migraines, and was going to set up a healing practice.

Still, this never felt quite right. Seemed to me, I wasn't healed enough or qualified enough.

More courses followed. And an empty bank account. And no well-paying job.

Hitting Bottom with the Spiritual Addiction

Fast forward to two years ago — I had been awake four days straight; my weight had dropped nine pounds; living in a state of terror, I attempted to commit suicide.

My husband took me to hospital. They put me under heavy sedation.

Back home, I realized finally that I was in spiritual addiction.

By Then, Recovery from Spiritual Addiction Was Very Hard

This recovery is not something I'm taking lightly. As I'm sure that others in recovery know, addiction is a living hell (although it doesn't start out that way).

While purposely coming back from the spiritual addiction, I came across Rose's website. I recognized that spiritual addiction was what had happened to me... as well as many problems related to being an unskilled empath.

By the time I found Rose's website, I was in spiritual shutdown. But, as you know if you have learned about Empath Empowerment®, trying to close yourself off from energies doesn't stop what Rose calls "Imported STUFF" from getting into an unskilled empath's aura.

Nor does trying to shut down energies take away other kinds of STUFF *already* in your aura.

What Got Me Through

Most important was my husband, my very amazing human husband. (He's not woo-woo at all.)

Also, finding Rose's website helped me understand what had happened to me.

I just wanted to go back to my very normal life, to shallow up and forget about angels, the Law of Attraction, being a Reiki master, and being an empath.

But the empath thing just wouldn't let up. So I knew I'd have to dip my toes back in, enough to get skills to turn my empath gifts OFF.

I'm taking my time with her books for empaths, and I know I need to do more than the "Empath's First Aid" technique in "The Empowered Empath."

I'm careful not to become obsessive about doing anything that Rose offers in her books. Instead I read instructions for a technique, do the technique, and end the technique.

After what happened, I struggle to connect to God. With that breakdown, I lost trust in everything, including my ability — or even my right — to connect to God.

These days I won't connect to angels at all, not even Archangels. I've had to work really hard to get me back and, two years after my breakdown, I'm still working on it.

—Marie Wilson, Melbourne, Australia

Rose Adds These Comments

Marie's cautionary tale has a happy ending. That's important to remember, Powerfully Human Reader. As I share her courageous words with you, I hope that you'll keep the rest of this perspective in mind:

1. New Age Spirituality is not the only path that can (and sometimes does) lead to spiritual addiction. I have helped clients from very diverse backgrounds to overcome

spiritual addiction: Christianity, Judaism, Buddhism, Hinduism, and more.

2.   Marie may have gained real benefit from everything that she tried to feel better. Seems to me, an imbalance in her lifestyle — that over-dependence on Technique Time — contributed significantly to the psychological drama.

3.   Other skill sets within RES can help a person to become more stable. Supplementing "The New Strong," you might consider others in the Energy HEALING Series and also the titles in the series called "An Empath Empowerment® Book."

4.   *This* book, like sessions with any RES expert, is not intended as a substitute for help from a mental health professional. In RES, we do not hold ourselves out as mental health professionals. But sometimes we can help people to *prevent* difficulties; especially what you have learned in this Program for Easy Vibrational Balance.

5.   Everyone living now, in the Age of Awakening transitional years, is more at risk than before for spiritual addiction. This vicious cycle can spin out of control, as happened to Marie. But this cycle is also something a person can stop.

In a way, it's heartening to consider that the **consciousness lifestyle** of spiritual addiction is a very real addiction.

Before the vicious cycle progresses very far, it's easier to change one's habits. Yet, however entrenched the habits, the consciousness lifestyle of human-based spirituality is always available.

3. From Spiritual Growth to Spiritual Addiction (And Back Again)

Rose, I can't thank you enough for your guidance in helping me: First, thanks for identifying that I even had a spiritual addiction. Second, you helped me to release it so quickly.

For as long as I can remember, I have been on a serious spiritual path... but over the past few decades, without realizing it, I picked up so many practices and found a way to integrate them ALL into every waking hour:

1. Emotional Freedom Technique (EFT)
2. Reiki
3. Tantric Buddhism
4. Hinduism
5. Kabbalah
6. Just to name just some of the highlights!!!

Seriously, a piece of every one of them became a part of my every waking hour, like a comfortable hum inside my head... whether I was chanting mantras... or visualizing symbols... or tapping.

I had convinced myself that they were adding to my spiritual growth, when in reality they were keeping me comfortably numb.

I actually enjoyed the comfortable, peaceful, floaty feeling I had grown accustomed to — that space of spiritual addiction.

Then you showed me how to simply drop the addiction and resume having a life!

Now My Spiritual Growth is Back on Track

I have been amazed at the level of connection I feel in my life now, in lieu of the all-consuming spiritual practices, chanting, mantras, etc.

Now I am so much more present, and I have a healthier balance with my spiritual growth. Life is lived as somebody who belongs on earth, in my body, mind, and soul.

I realize now that spiritual addiction was actually keeping me stuck in the same place I'd been accustomed to for the past decade — nothing like the growth I originally set out to attain.

— Robin Rodriguez, Scranton, Pennsylvania

4. The Last Thing
I Thought I'd Be Learning,
How to Have Fun

My life used to be defined by "working on myself." In fact, introspection became a serious lifestyle, taking precedence over actual living.

I thought that was what I needed to do in order to become everything I was capable of becoming. I was always valiantly engaged in some sort of self-analysis and emotional work, or meditation, or other self-help practice.

This felt deep and meaningful. It seemed like I was gaining so much insight and making so much progress. And yet I still struggled with so many old issues. For the full-time job I made it into, I was not getting the transformational results I hoped for, and actually became more tied-up inside.

Never would I have predicted how much better I'd feel by limiting my Technique Time to just 20 minutes a day. Here are some of the changes:

- Now I no longer live inside my head, monitoring and manipulating my thoughts and emotions in order to feel better.
  Letting go of that unnatural burden was an immediate relief, but there were other pleasant surprises too.

- I started noticing that I was getting more respect at work, and I gained a reputation for being capable and trustworthy at my job.

- What happened when I could enjoy regular interactions without feeling like every conversation had to be a deep-sea dive into the psyche? I began seeing my friends more.

- I learned I can exercise my full range of positioning awareness in everyday life, from shallow to deep. And with good old human shallow as the default!

- Since I gained a lot more time to do some actual living, I've even discovered some new hobbies.

Looking back, my time in spiritual addiction was extremely lonely and isolating, like living locked inside my mind with nothing more concrete than my own thoughts and feelings to keep me company.

Leaving behind that consciousness lifestyle was like opening the blinds and letting the sunshine in. Not just sunshine, actually, but friends, and a new zest for my life, and more success at work, and so much more fun.

— Hannah Martin, Toronto, Canada

5. Enjoying
The Opposite of Chaos

Used to be, my relationships were based on energy. Everywhere I went, first I read people's energies: Family, friends, workplace, customers, strangers, store staff, you name it. This was chaos. I dreaded being around people and noticed myself becoming awfully stuck in life.

Consciously choosing to not be focused on energies has brought relief and empowerment. The biggest change was at work. I used to be quiet and accepting of everyone else's ways, bottling anger within me so I could avoid energies of friction. That also meant doing a majority of the work, while others took on the leftovers.

Now I speak up for myself and ask others to take on more.

Stepping away from spiritual addiction has allowed me the freedom to be aware of my human wants and needs. I know when I am mad. Or hungry. Or doing too much. Or feeling lonely.

And now I can notice when other people try to take advantage of me. Then I take appropriate action in objective reality, saying things and doing things to stick up for myself.

In recovering from spiritual addiction, the biggest thing I have gained is self-empowerment. It's like I'm living the opposite of chaos. What is that? Something quite simple. You see, I'm just naturally living my human life.

— Kenji Yamada, New York, New York

6. Why Those Veeeerrrrry Long Pauses?

To discover I had spiritual addiction was the best thing that could possibly have happened to me. Sounds strange, but it's totally true.

From an early age I was a spiritual seeker. And, God, did I feel as if I did not belong to this world! My spiritual journey continued year after year and:

1. I didn't reach enlightenment
2. I didn't feel more comfortable as a human being
3. I felt c-r-a-z-y.

What else did I feel? A growing uneasiness, more fear, more strange thoughts, more brain fog, and much more confusion.

Mixed in with this were some very happy moments, like when my Law of Attraction practice paid off and I got what I wanted.

Feeling encouraged, I practiced yoga, Emotional Freedom Technique, and several different kinds of meditation.

Then I began sensing energies all day long.

Encouraged, I thought my uncomfortable feelings would go away if only I did even *more* healing, more meditation practice, etc.

Then I did some research on "New Age" and found Rose's blog, something quite different and more empowering.

I'm amazed that she came across the subtle pattern of positioning consciousness that she calls "spiritual addiction." It is still a mystery to me how one can become so skilled as an aura reader. (For sure, I want to learn this skill eventually.)

Based on what I read online, I set up a Skype session with Rose. At first she asked me some questions that were standard for a first session. Then Rose surprised me. She asked why it took me so long to answer these simple questions. She said I had made veeeerrrrry long pauses.

That was because it was hard for me to say what I wanted to say. Or even *know* what I wanted to say. As usual, talking about myself felt like searching in an unknown land, and I wanted to find the very perfect right answer.

Rose explained that every time I made these long pauses, I took a visit to the astral. I was totally shocked.

In this particular session, for the first time, I really understood in a personal way what spiritual addiction meant: what it had to do with me and my behavior.

Making long pauses when being asked simple questions? I stopped doing that. I began saying the first thing that came into my mind, no more waiting. Quite a change!

By now it has been a year since I began following Rose's recommendations — 20 Minutes of Technique Time, Tops — and also doing some of the simple RES techniques for self-healing.

Never before have I felt this human and grounded. Nor have I ever felt this balanced before. And effective. And practical. I'm even showing signs of being clever in a *human* kind of way. Most important, never before have I felt this much like myself.

So I can't thank Rose enough for opening my eyes. For real.

— Maximilian Reiter, Vienna, Austria

7. Satisfyingly Messy

In 2009 I had full-blown spiritual addiction. I was floating about trying to find what spirit wanted for me, doing healing techniques like tapping (Emotional Freedom Technique), reading my energy constantly through the day, etc.

At the same time, my real life was falling apart. I lost my job because I wasn't focused on it. (Instead I was daydreaming about my perfect life.)

Then I tried to start my own business as a coach/healer. The money just wasn't coming in. When I did work with clients, I felt so drained afterwards that I wouldn't be able to do anything else for the rest of the day.

My health was suffering as I tried to eat an extreme "pure" diet because it was more "spiritual."

Sadly, that wasn't all. I got to the point where I had to phone my mum to ask her for help with my mortgage payment.

And then one day my husband came home and said he couldn't stand it anymore, living with this floaty, impractical person. He asked for a divorce.

That was the wake-up I needed. I had a phone session with Rose, which helped me to move into what she now calls "human-based spirituality."

Next, I started focusing on my real life and got a job. While it didn't pay well, I worked hard and learned a lot of new skills. After a year I was taken on permanently, plus they doubled my salary.

My husband and I went to counselling. Seven years on, our relationship is wonderful. During that time, I had some sessions with Rose and read her blog, learned some energy healing skills through her books, and also began to use her skills for Empath Empowerment®.

Is this next part obvious? I stopped constantly reading my own energies and everyone else's! There's plenty to notice in objective reality.

What else? I learned to use real-life skills like "Saying No" and "Use Your Words, Alice." These work considerably better than trying to fix the energies of a situation.

It's not been linear progress. There have been periods when I stopped doing my 20 Daily Minutes of Technique Time. Not coincidentally, I would start slipping back into my old ways of reading energy throughout the day.

When this happens, I recognize it much more quickly now, and can get back to a routine that suits me better.

In "Conversations with God" by Neale Donaldson Walsh, there's a part where God says, "I am the profound and the profane." This is what I like about Rosetree Energy Spirituality: your spiritual growth is not enhanced by separating from the messy reality of human life. Instead you grow faster by fully engaging with what it means to be human.

— Alice Roberts, Berkshire, England

CHAPTER 26

Your Role in Healing Our Awakening World

Now that I have learned so much about The New Strong, how can I give back?

That's a fair question. Beyond fair, generous.

But that is so typical of you, Powerfully Human Reader. Such a question reveals a deeply spiritual quality of aspiration. One that has motivated a lot of your choices in life, hasn't it?

Even your choice to explore this Program for Easy Vibrational Balance. Sure, you wanted to keep yourself safe. And maybe you sensed that better vibrational positioning could help you attain a higher state of consciousness, even Enlightenment. (True.)

Yet tickling the back of your mind, tucked softly into your heart, didn't you also wish to become stronger so that you could help others?

This time of transition after The Shift really is a doozy. Millions are stuck in spiritual addiction or psychological overwork or spiritual shutdown. (Or chemical addiction where, depending on the substance of choice, the person gets deeply stuck in either spiritual addiction or spiritual shutdown.)

Through your example you can do a great deal to help others. Consider it a form of spiritual service, living on earth as a person who isn't too proud to be human.

Superb auric modeling, I call it. This hidden aspect of your life is subconsciously evident to every person you meet. Although at the level of conscious, human thinking, what will be noticed? Nothing special.

Okay, maybe this. You seem like somebody who acts with integrity. Or substitute different language if you like, Powerfully Human Reader. What words do you use to describe when someone is spiritually balanced without bragging about it?

That way. You have learned how to live that way. And you may keep it your own personal business, how self-healing techniques in our program have included some skills for co-creating with the Divine.

As you complete this book, at this particular time in your life, what about your future? What's going to be your next project? Perhaps your 20 Daily Minutes of Technique Time, Tops will include learning even more techniques for co-creating with God.

Otherwise, vibrationally balanced living in this Age of Awakening is plenty. You're doing a new kind of Divine co-creation in everyday life. This demands nothing special from you, other than taking an interest in your human life and doing what makes you happy.

Might I compare this auric modeling to having a physical shadow? When was the last time you had to work hard at that?

Okay, shadows aren't usually symbols of light but of darkness. Look, here's the point I'm trying to make. On earth, our shadows show. How hilarious is that? Your grime-colored shadow. That is what shows.

Every day of your life, that shadow has been on display, emanating from your physical body.

Meanwhile, how about the hidden light of your aura? Have you ever wondered, why doesn't that show instead? That energy field of yours is so much sweeter, so why isn't that the part that shows?

Your Magnificent Energy Field

How magnificent now, your aura! Snugly tucked around your human-frequency body, it fits you perfectly, especially now, with that snazzy human-based consciousness lifestyle, and cleaned up with your new skills. Your aura includes:

- Divine-level perfection, unchanging gifts of your soul that will last throughout this entire lifetime.

- Astral-level evolution, the ever-changing displays of your spiritual and emotional growth.

- It's delicious enough to make you blush — or would be, if only you fully perceived just how gorgeous your aura is now.

- And always this is your special brand of gorgeousness, totally distinctive.

Just how big and bright is it really? While being human, do people like us ever know the full story?

Karen Watching Her Cat

One of my students, Karen Kline, told me this story about her cat.

One of my cats died. I happened to be there right as his spirit left his body.

The spirit of my cat was so big. So colorful. It was full of wisdom and joy.

The spirit of my cat was enormous. How could such an enormous spirit body have been contained in my little cat?

I couldn't wrap my mind around it. Still, I'm so glad that I saw this. It changed my life.

You know what else? I'm glad I only saw it at the end. What if, all along, I had known about this spirit of my cat? How could I have treated him in a normal way? I would have been so self-conscious.

The Best Human Illusion of All

Powerfully Human Reader, besides that neat cat trick, Earth School brings us many other amazing illusions. Some have been explored in this book.

Beneath those illusions, what's true? Spiritually you are a vast being. So is every other human on earth.

As with Karen's cat, that physical body of yours is only a fraction of the whole.

Not that I recommend you walk around all day long, searching for your outermost edges. By now you surely know this! But how about doing this quick experiment now, just for a moment?

One Last, Tiny Bit of Technique Time

Powerfully Human Reader, it's your final graduation present. Give a quick read to the following steps. Then *do* them, opening your eyes to peek at instructions as needed:

1. Close your eyes and picture yourself like "My cup runneth over" in the 23rd psalm.

2. Let your body be that cup. Feel it brimming over, how you are co-creating with God.

3. The distinctive essence of the person you are right now — experience that actively as joy, as peace, as love, as power, however you like. That is what brims over and out, your Divine-level way of blessing this world.

4. Ultimately that effortless kind of perfection is your distinctive contribution to this universe. Your full set of subtle energy bodies, each one nesting inside the next, and all of it brimming over. A unique, unpredictable wonder... this is who you are energetically, a creative miracle.

5. Open your eyes. Let that kind of reality go, the energy part, and return to identifying yourself as a Powerfully Human Reader.

Okay, Back to Human Business as Usual

Outside of Technique Time, you can well afford to go back to your human job. All 10 of the New Vibrational Rules on earth could be summarized this way: *Live without apology, doing your human best.*

Will your light inspire others? Have no doubt about that. Those who can be inspired consciously, yes, they will be inspired. What about those who can't? Not your responsibility.

Dare to be human and you will evolve so fast, both psychologically and spiritually. Automatically, you can heap glories on glories, doing spiritual service for as long as you live in this so-sacred world.

Join with me and all who recognize this great spiritual privilege. Living at this turning point in the vibrational history of Earth, we have a God-golden opportunity for growth within ourselves, as well as service to others.

In all the unfathomable possibility of what can be, ever, this magnificent chance will never come again.

Acknowledgments

My heartfelt gratitude goes to all the apprentices and graduates in the Mentoring Program for RES. You know who you are, so-talented people who are moving this system forward into the world!

Respected colleagues in mind-body-spirit, working in other modalities, I am so grateful to you as well. Each of us has an important role to play in this Age of Awakening.

Next, I am grateful to Teaching of the Inner Christ (TIC), including what they taught me about ET healing. This gave me a frame of reference for adapting the knowledge and skills taught to me by the Reverend AlixSandra Parness and the Reverend Rich Bell, back during the Age of Faith.

Beyond that, TIC taught me to purposely co-create with the Divine. Which is how I have written this book and every single book I've published since 1986. Such huge gratitude!

For "Lock the Door, Hide the Key," I acknowledge the influence of two great systems for self-healing, Donna Eden's Energy Medicine and The Body Code System by Dr. Bradley Nelson. Adapting one technique from each system, ("Zip Up" and "Shields Up," respectively) I have added, subtracted, and vibrationally positioned.

Judy Lavine, the medical intuitive and energy healer, introduced me to "Align with Mother Earth." This, too, I have adapted with gratitude.

For this book, special thanks are due to Nigel Yorwerth, Peter Bowerman, Peri Gabriel, Dana Wheeler, Mitch Weber, and Matthew Weber. Further acknowledgment goes to Lou deSabla and Erin deSabla of Pathways Magazine, where I write a column on "Energetic Literacy."

If you live in the nation's capital, you know it's no Sedona. Special grit is required to support our mind-body-spirit community. Lou has maintained this visionary publication for 40 years, and always with such integrity.

Being of service in the Age of Awakening is humbling, challenging, and the greatest privilege I can imagine. To all the Divine Beings who have helped and inspired me, and to those irreplaceable humans who have lit my way, I stand here in such gratitude.

Continue Your
Discoveries with The New Strong

At Rose Rosetree's Website You'll Find

- Annotated Table of Contents
- Glossary
- Index

Other Goodies? Galore!

- Join the lively informal online community at Rose's blog (30,000 comments and counting): "Deeper Perception Made Practical."
- Sign up for the free monthly e-newsletter, "Reading Life Deeper."
- Take Rose's Workshop for The New Strong Read the juicy details at the part of Rose's website where workshops are listed. Decide if this unique group experience is for you!
- More books by Rose Rosetree are available to teach you energy READING skills, energy HEALING skills, Empath Empowerment®. There's even Enlightenment Coaching.

www.rose-rosetree.com

Dear Reader:

Suddenly here we are at the end of this book! You have begun to live The New Strong. Those Seven Success Stories near the end? In the future, you may discover one that is even more inspiring — the New Strong Story of Your Own.

The fun is just starting for you, I hope. Might I ask a favor that will help spread this fun around?

As an independent writer, I strive to develop skills and teach them and test them and write them up and rewrite and do seemingly endless edits and, finally, typeset and publish. But there's one thing I cannot do, and that is called "Book reviews."

Here is where you can make such a difference. Book reviews are the single most important way to help others find a good book. Especially a book like this one, written in an upstairs bedroom (my little pink office) by somebody who runs a one-person publishing company.

Please write a review of this book, then share it at Amazon.com, barnesandnoble.com, goodreads.com, and any other book review venues you know. If you have a blog or belong to a group online, maybe cut-and-paste your book review there, too.

A review need not be long. Even a couple of sentences can make such a difference for other people who are seeking this kind of knowledge and don't know where to find it.

You'll also be giving back in a way that makes such a difference to me personally. I strive to bring innovation to spiritual self-help... and do it with integrity.

Thank you for joining me. You have learned leading-edge techniques, making you a co-pioneer with this Program for Easy Vibrational Balance. It has been my honor to guide you and give you the best that I have to offer. Stay in touch at my blog, if you like. Above all, I wish you such happiness!

Bye for now,

Rose Rosetree

About the Author

Rose Rosetree is America's leading-edge expert on reading the human energy field. Author of the international bestseller "Aura Reading through All Your Senses," her work with energetic literacy has been reported in *The Los Angeles Times*, *The Washington Post*, and *USA Today*.

Altogether she has given over 1,000 media interviews, speaking to broadcasters as varied as Diane Rehm, Steve Doocy, and the ladies of "The View."

Working with clients and students worldwide, Rose has developed six trademarked skill sets for energy HEALING as well as energy READING.

As the founder of Rosetree Energy Spirituality (RES), Rose has twice broken records for being the most popular energy healer in the history of VOICE, Japan's foremost seminar company. Now you can benefit from her expertise by using the revolutionary skill sets designed to help you live... The New Strong.

CPSIA information can be obtained
at www.ICGtesting.com
Printed in the USA
FFOW01n0729100616
24799FF